My Testament to the UN

A Contribution to the 50th Anniversary
of the United Nations

1995

by

Robert Muller

WORLD HAPPINESS and COOPERATION
P.O. Box 1153
Anacortes, Washington 98221
U.S.A.

1992

My Testament to the UN

by

Robert Muller

Published by
World Happiness and Cooperation
P.O. Box 1153
Anacortes, Washington 98221
U.S.A.

First Edition - December, 1992

Library of Congress Catalog Card Number: 92-062634

ISBN   1-880455-07-1

Table of Contents

My Testament to the UN

by

Robert Muller

1

The UN and a New Civilization

This testament was started on an April's fool day (1 April, 1984). Isn't it up to all of us, including you dear reader, to transform our wildest dreams of humanity into realities? This is what the UN is all about.

*

Like the spring of a New Era, a new philosophy, spirituality and global civilization are slowly but surely emerging from the UN. This is visible only to a few people today, but in the next century it will be crystal-clear to all.

*

As we celebrate the fortieth and each successive anniversary of the UN, we must remember all those who for more than 2000 years, beginning with Confucius, the Buddha, Jesus and the Greeks have dreamt of a united human family and later of a league of nations. Among the latter were Abbé de St Pierre, Benjamin Franklin, Simon Bolivar, Immanuel Kant, Andrew Carnegie, Woodrow Wilson and last but not least Franklin Roosevelt who completed the historical process on American soil.

*

The only limits of the UN are our doubts and hesitations of today.

*

The UN is now universal. Practically all nations of Earth are members of it. This is unprecedented in human history. The divine plan of one place on Earth where all nations would meet has materialized. As Pope Paul VI said:

"You are the end of a journey which started 2000 years ago."

*

Einstein predicted:

"We shall require a substantially new manner of thinking if humankind is to survive."

No organization on Earth has contributed more to a new thinking than the UN.

*

An isolationist American group has published a pamphlet:

A World without the UN."

Strangely enough its cover shows the UN emerging from an egg, symbol of birth rather than demise.

*

Through the UN humanity progressively acquires a collective way of looking at things, thus entering a new phase of evolution: the phase of planethood, the global age.

*

At the beginning the UN was only a hope.

Today it is a political reality.

Tomorrow it will be the world's religion.

*

The UN is the most important new moral force in the world. Historians will some day be astonished by its role in ushering humanity into the third millennium.

*

The most important division on this planet is not between East and West and between North and South. The most important division is between those who want human unity and world order and those who want the supremacy of their group at the expense of the planet and of humanity.

*

The faith, love and hope of humanity are waiting for something new: a great, beautiful vision of what this world could be. It is the role of the UN to fashion that image as a normal step in the evolution of this planet, as a collective mould of the dreams, perceptions and experiences of all peoples.

*

In the new era of peace, all humans must be respected as divine manifestations of the universe, as unique, unrepeatable cosmic units endowed with the absolute right not to kill and not to be killed, not even in the name of a nation.

*

We will henceforth live in a world obsessed with peace and demilitarization until these objectives are achieved. And they will be achieved sooner than we dare to think.

*

Peace, order, justice, equity, freedom, well-being and happiness are basic human cravings. The UN is the first attempt ever to achieve these aims world-wide. It is one of the greatest advances in human evolution.

*

History tells us that what seems utopian today will be a reality tomorrow. That reality will depend on what we do for utopia at the UN today.

*

"As all associations aim at some good, that association which is the most sovereign among them all and embraces all others will aim highest, i.e. at the most sovereign of all goods."

Aristotle

This could be the definition of the UN.

*

These words of the prophet Isaiah apply to the UN:
"Do not destroy it, for there is a blessing in it."

*

The present human society is a product of the past and also a producer of the future. The UN and its agencies are the main harbingers of that future.

*

Confucius said that forty is the age of consolidation. The UN, thank God, has been able to reach that age, twice the age of its defunct predecessor, the League of Nations.

*

The UN is the center of things, the vortex, the point of convergence of human evolution. It is the first and sole political institution on Earth that cares for the entire planet and for all humanity. And these are the two fundamental imperatives of our time.

*

Due to the fast growing irrelevance and harmfulness of national sovereignty in a global world that cries out for care and proper management, we live in a negative sociological era. The UN is the only cradle of hope for a new, positive era.

*

We are all *"pontifices maximi"*, great bridge-builders. Our most important duty at this stage is to communicate, to exchange ideas, to adapt, to seek, to try, to network, to learn to evolve in a global environment. Perhaps the greatest contribution of the UN is to be a place on Earth where all nations can talk to each other, learn from each other and engage into the most comprehensive socratic dialogue ever.

*

The UN is sometimes called a jungle. Yes, it is as rich and life-teeming as a jungle, for it reflects the richness, bio-diversity and complexity of our planetary home and human beings. It is a perfect mirror of the cosmic realities of our planet.

*

The UN is the first significant victory over war. That victory will soon be decisive.

*

The UN sometimes seems to me one vast planetary prayer, interspersed with many sins and falls.

The UN is the New Genesis.

*

The UN's tall glass building elevates high into the sky the dreams, hopes and loves of humanity, and channels down to Earth the cosmic messages of God and of the universe.

*

The UN is a new paradigm, probably the greatest ever in human history. It is the product and instrument of very deep evolutionary changes. Its role has accelerated in the last decades. For nations, for religions, for business, for the media, for educators, for professions, for all peoples of the Earth there is nothing more important than to find out what emerges from this first world-wide global observatory, warning-tower and light-house of planet Earth.

*

The UN is the sole universal organization on Earth. What luck that we have at least one above the myriads of national, local and group establishments!

*

The fundamental tasks of the UN are to ensure peace and justice, to provide planetary information, to develop planetary consciousness, to give voice to planetary concerns, to create planetary networks, to issue planetary warnings, to establish planetary institutions, to organize planetary events and to pave the way to proper planetary governance. No institution on Earth has ever had such mind-boggling tasks.

*

If there is one accomplishment humanity can be proud of, it is the UN.

*

It is the UN's lofty, unprecedented role to transform the whole world into a peaceful, well-ordered society. It is the world's greatest peace engine. Its imperfections will be corrected and forgotten with time.

*

Archbishop Helder Camara said to me:

"I love the United Nations, it does such an important work. Pope Paul VI also loved the UN and once commented to me: 'Of course it has its defects and makes mistakes. But doesn't the Catholic Church have its defects too and haven't we made many mistakes over the last 2000 years?' And doesn't this apply to many other groups and efforts on this planet?"

He then embraced me and said:

"God bless the United Nations"

These were the same words of Pope John Paul II when he visited the United Nations.

*

Imperfect UN? Why not? How could it be otherwise? Given the national differences and idiosyncrasies of this planet, how could a first, small, powerless organization, dealing with all the miseries of our Earth be perfect? Its critics must be joking.

*

If the big powers continue with their hesitation towards the UN, it is quite possible that they will miss one of the greatest opportunities ever in history: the creation of the first universal world order.

*

Everything on this Earth becomes "organized" or "institutionalized", for it is the way of the human species. This is true both of good and evil, of love and hatred. The great challenge of our time is to institutionalize and organize well-being and cooperation on a planetary scale and to de-institutionalize war and hatred. This is the deeper meaning of the United Nations.

*

The dinosaurs disappeared from the Earth possibly because their brains were too small. The human race may also disappear if it does not develop its global brain - the UN - to the required size.

*

The people of the world are left without a sense of direction. They are assaulted every day by torrents of news, views, values, marketing and advertisements. Their life is not whole. The human society is not whole. The United Nations is the only place on Earth which can give humanity a new sense of direction, a general holistic philosophy and vision of a global, planetary civilization.

*

All people in the world want the same things: peace, justice, good health and a happy, satisfying life.

All people in the world strive for the same things: they study and work hard to obtain the good things in life.

All peoples in the world abhor the same things: war, violence, injustice, sickness, poverty, lack of freedom, etc.

It is no little achievement that humanity at long last has defined what it wants and what it rejects. We are now trying to achieve these objectives for all humanity. That is the great historical challenge of our time, the duty of our generation and the momentous task of the UN. May all people of the world make it their objective too, and be members of the UN whose Charter begins with the words:

"We, the Peoples of the United Nations..."
*

Is it possible that despite our thousands of years of history, our religions, our research, our sciences, our penetration into the infinitely large and infinitely small, humankind has never really tried to understand the meaning of life? Yes, it is quite possible. It is even a fact.

Is it possible that we have never tried to understand the history of the universe and of our role in it? Yes, it is quite possible. It is even a fact.

Is it possible that seeing now this Earth as one globe, knowing all its elements, resources and limits, no one is wondering how it should be managed, cared for, preserved and loved? Yes, it is quite possible. It is even a fact.

Is it possible that having lived so long and knowing fairly well our paleontology, archaeology and history, no one is trying to visualize seriously the future? Yes, it is quite possible. This too is even a fact.

Well, if all this is possible, is it not vital that someone should come along who would do it for us? Yes, and this someone is the UN and its agencies, nurtured by all cultures, beliefs, learning, experiences and efforts of all nations, by the hopes, dreams and faith of all people, by the thoughts of all great men and women, living and dead.

And is it possible that you and I have a responsibility and role to play? Yes, it is possible. It is even certain.

Therefore we should know the UN, care for the UN, preach the UN, teach the UN, love the UN and advocate the UN until our death and even beyond.

Yes, the UN is just and necessary.

*

History, evolution are nothing but the slow progressive flowering of all Earth people into full humaneness. Cultures are the ways and means of that progress. Today, in a world become global, the United Nations is the first momentous attempt to fashion a world culture of peace, justice and humaneness for all.

*

The UN reflects the stage and dynamics of human progress:

- As a universal political organization it is the culmination of 2000 years of history and dreams for a world organization;

- While war has always been the rule in history, the UN asserts peace as the dominant new rule of civilized behavior;

- The UN has begun the decisive battle against armaments, the military and violence;

- It has subdued the trade and financial rivalries which have led to so many wars;

- It has started novel histories of world cooperation in development, the environment, education, health, outer-space, the seas and oceans, population, children, women, the handicapped, the elderly, races, etc;

- It has started the world-wide defense and protection of individual human rights;

Feeble and unsupported as it is, the UN will some day receive the universal, astonished acclaim and thanks of the human race.

*

Why do I feel so at ease and happy in the UN? Because it is the place on Earth where the world's problems are being worked out. It is the great, new, exciting frontier of human progress. I see the UN as Columbus saw a new shore.

*

If power is defined as the ability to create the stage and the script in which others will act, then the UN is certainly the most powerful organization on Earth.

If influence is the new power, then the UN is again the most powerful organization on Earth.

*

Humanity must frontally and seriously attack the problem of violence in all its forms:

Violent action
Violent speech and communications
Violent thoughts

We therefore need a science and art of peace to vigorously promote:

Peaceful behavior and actions
Peaceful speech and communications
Peaceful thoughts

The UN and its agencies are humanity's first universal instruments of peace and non-violence.

*

The UN is an unprecedented world-wide effort to make humanity think in unison, care in unison, feel in unison, act in unison, in other words to become unison (unisono: the same sound), i.e. one united nation.

*

We must love the UN with a fire in our heart, the fire of the upcoming human and planetary unity, the fire of a new, world-wide, peaceful human society.

*

A reader quotes these words of U Thant:

"The Charter of the United Nations is the first, most daring code of behavior addressed to the most powerful of all institutions of this planet: armed nations."

And she continues:

"Many disappointments have led people to question the value of the United Nations but much of this skepticism is the result of lack of understanding about what the UN can and cannot do. As U Thant said, the Charter is a "code of behavior", not a constitution with the force of law. It can only be effective if the signatories live up to its terms".

*

The UN should be loved for its defense of the great causes of humanity. Even its weaknesses and failures should be loved, as we love the weaknesses and frailties of a child.

*

The UN is the cradle of universal human values and truths on our global, cosmic journey.

*

The UN is the greatest school or laboratory on Earth for the study of entities and their relationships in a universal and total time dimension.

*

All the great truths of our cosmic journey and planetary evolution will emerge from the UN. Few are those on Earth who fathom its evolutionary importance.

*

The United Nations Charter will survive and gain incessant ground in the world, even if the UN should disappear. The Oath of Strasbourg between the sons of Charlemagne, forerunner of the European Community, survived Lotharingia and all Franco-German wars. The Magna Carta survived feudalism and blossomed centuries later into the Declarations of Independence and Human Rights. The Declaration of Human Rights survived the French Revolution and Napoleon. Similarly, the UN Charter and declarations will survive and win. And history will be astonished how rapidly this will take place. The UN is scoring victory after victory for independence, for peace, for development, for freedom, for justice, for quality of life, for the environment, for human rights, for racial equality, for the rights of women, of children, of the elderly, of the handicapped, etc. Even the most stubborn contemporary issues, namely the cold war, armaments, militarism and national sovereignty have or will succumb to the power of this new bold paradigm. The UN is the latest and greatest landmark in the ascent, progress and further evolution of humankind towards the fulfillment of its intended role on this miraculous planet in the vast universe.

*

Right here, right now, this planet is our heaven, our paradise, our home. It is time that all humans and entities realize it, be well educated and informed about it and take good care of it.

*

What is the pattern, what is the philosophy, what is the great stream of upward thought and vision that should guide our next phase of evolution?

The answer will come from humanity's biggest crucible of thoughts: the United Nations.

*

This text addressed to Jerusalem applies, as well, to the United Nations, the new Jerusalem:

"Rise up in splendor, your light has come, the glory of God shines upon you. See, darkness covers the Earth and thick clouds cover the peoples; but upon you the Lord shines, and over you appears His glory. Nations shall walk by your light, and kings by your shining radiance. Raise your eyes and look about: they all gather and come to you; your sons come from afar, and your daughters in the arms of their nurses. Then you shall be radiant at what you see, your heart shall throb and overflow, for the riches of the sea shall be emptied out before you, the wealth of nations shall be

14

brought to you. Caravans of people shall fill you, coming from East and West, from North and South, bearing gold and frankincense, and proclaiming the praises of the Lord."

Isaiah

*

"Dag Hammarsjköld once predicted that the day would come when people would see the United Nations for what it really is, not the abstract painting of some artist, but a drawing done by the peoples of the world. It is not the perfect institution of the dreamers who saw it as the only true road to world harmony, and not the evil instrument of world domination that the isolationists once made it out to be."

Henry Kissinger

*

The UN, the eternal human dreams at long last incarnated in a political institution of planetary dimension, and in its living servants.

*

It is strange that we have not even asked ourselves the fundamental questions on this planet, namely: what is our purpose? What does the cosmos or God have in mind for us? Why are we born, why do we die? Since leaders and thinkers do not ask themselves these questions, the world is in disarray. It is high time to start that debate on a planetary scale, benefiting from the perceptions, beliefs and best minds of all cultures. We need a UN world conference on the meaning of life and another on the meaning of death.

*

The UN is the most momentous event in modern history. It is the first universal political instrument which makes us realize that we are universal beings.

*

If the UN did not exist, it would have to be invented.

*

The UN is a living model of the search for peace on this planet.

*

Few believed in past centuries that slavery could be abolished.
Yet, it was abolished.

Few believe in this century that armaments can be abolished.
Yet, they will be abolished.

Few believe that militarism can be suppressed.
Yet, it will be suppressed.

Few believe that national sovereignty will disappear.
Yet, it will disappear.

*

"If there is an evolution, however slow, in the direction of world community, it will probably owe a great deal to the presence of thousands of trained people in every part of the globe whose calling as diplomats requires them to look over their own fence in an effort to understand how other peoples' minds and consciences work.

In a world of more than 160 nation-states, the number of potential armed conflicts is far greater than the number of those that have actually broken out. Diplomacy must be judged by what it prevents and not only by what it achieves. Much of it is a holding action designed to avoid explosion until the unifying forces of history take us into their embrace."

Abba Eban

*

The tremendous symbolism of the birthplace of the UN:

San Francisco:
St. Francis, the saint of the poor, of peace, of the environment and of joy.

The Mission of Madre de las Dolores:
The Mother of Pains, the UN born in pains.

Indeed, the UN reflects the birth of a new society: an interdependent, world-wide human society. Like any birth, it takes place in pain and in joy and only the joy will be remembered.

*

The crazy, chaotic, incomprehensible world of today is but a giant evolutionary readjustment in search for higher world-wide human fulfillment and a better world society. We will all gain from the process.

*

There is a philosophy of peace, justice, development and quality of life emerging from the UN. In the past, religions, kings and nations enlisted God to justify their cause and sanctify their path: Abraham came down from the mountain, proclaiming: "*God is with us*!" Moses got the ten commandments from God. Mohammed read the Koran straight from the lips of God. The Germans fought under the motto "*Gott mit uns*" and the Russians with "*Bog snami*".

Today, nations, rulers, religions and many causes try to enlist the UN, "The UN mit uns", but when one group succeeds, the losers proclaim: "The UN is no good."

*

Immense, deep, incredible changes are taking place on this planet and in the human society. They all press for peace, cooperation and a sense of wonder at our beautiful planet and at the miracle of life.

*

Why don't people realize that the UN is one of the greatest, most exciting, unprecedented new frontiers of human endeavors? Study the UN and its specialized agencies and you will see with fascination our current transformation, hopes, life forces at work and metamorphosis. The UN might well be called the Great Transformation.

*

"It is to the spirit and mind of man, to his ideas and his attitudes that we must devote considerable attention if the peace is going to be truly won. Unless we secure the right conditions for spiritual and intellectual health and unless we determine the right positive ideas for which we should live, I am afraid all our work may prove to have been in vain."

Ambassador Charles Malik
Signer of the original UN Charter

*

Day after day, thanks to the UN, our epoch is becoming one of growing international understanding, cooperation and friendship.

Our present, turbulent era is but the childhood of human unity. The UN is its kindergarten.

*

Centers of power and influence never remain the same. There were Egypt, Athens, Rome, Spain, London, and Paris. Today, there are Moscow and Washington. They never last, because power is unable to adapt itself to new evolutionary trends. Power believes it will always remain and that it must do everything to remain. It then misses evolution and falls aside it. Power is locked into its own internal and external logic, incapable of lifting itself into new trends, visions and solutions. In my view, the powerless UN is the great new womb of evolutionary change and adaptation on this planet, the nations' only chance to survive.

*

Fundamental questions of our time:

- What are the main trends and reasons of world evolution, past, present and future?
- What is the universe trying to achieve on this planet?
- What is the meaning of our senses, of our consciousness, of our mind, now vastly expanded by science and technology?
- Why do we want to know, why do we want to change this planet?
- How are we going to manage this Earth and the human society in times to come?

These questions are beginning to be raised in the UN. They must be accelerated urgently.

*

No one can stop evolution. However giant a power may be, whatever cause it might defend, whatever missiles and arms it may possess in the air, on the seas, in the soils and in the heavens, it will not be able to counter evolution. On the contrary, non-adaptation will cause its demise like that of the dinosaurs.

A new world is being born in the UN.

*

UN lamentation:
"Oh, my children, how can you ever forget that 30 million dead were my father and the atom bomb my mother?"

*

The UN is the only realistic hope left for this planet. It is rightly called the "House of Hope".

*

We are all instruments of the great march of time. We do not see the strategy and the direction, but we are all part of it. Out of trends the UN will fashion destiny.

*

If we believe in the rising tide of evolution and of human destiny, all nations and peoples will gain and rise. This is the cornerstone of the United Nations.

*

It is not the US, Russia, freedom or equality which are at stake. The entire human anthill is at stake.

*

When the famous Glenn Miller orchestra performed at the UN to celebrate the UN's fortieth anniversary and its own forty-fifth anniversary, they played *"Sentimental Journey"*, *"Serenade in Blue"*, and *"Rhapsody in Blue"*. I thanked them and said:

"As you played those tunes I was thinking that despite many dark days and pitfalls, the UN is the greatest sentimental journey on Earth, the journey towards universal love for our planet and humanity. That despite many thorny bushes, the UN is a serenade in blue chanting the Garden of Eden on Earth. That despite many false notes, the UN is a rhapsody in blue in the vast starry universe.

May God allow you to come back in 1995 to celebrate the UN's fiftieth anniversary and in the year 2000 to celebrate the Bimillennium. May our great sentimental journal be completed by that time, enabling us to hold the most beautiful world-wide Bimillennium Celebration of Life ever on this planet."

*

Ethical rules do not relate only to behavior between nations. They relate to God's whole Creation: our planetary home, our animal brothers, the heavens and the stars, ourselves.

*

Years ago when I was stationed in Geneva, I prayed that the world would produce another Montesquieu, Voltaire or Rousseau to guide humanity on its way. Today I realize that they were products of their time, of their history and of the notorious role of their countries. Today the only place on Earth which can produce the right new thinkers, world philosophers and visionaries is the United Nations. Dag Hammarskjöld and U Thant were the first.

*

How come that nations have such difficulty to unite for good, common causes and have such astonishing resourcefulness and endless imagination for division and destruction? Huge armaments and the vast national military establishments on the one hand and the poor little UN on the other hand, dramatically illustrate this evolutionary aberration. What a loss of precious time we indulge in!

*

The UN is the first organization in history which defends, world wide, the rights of the Earth, of humanity and of the individual. This is its sacred role, its threefold agenda. UN documents should start with the words:

> In the name of the Earth
> In the name of humanity
> In the name of the human person.

*

Someone sent me a horoscope of the UN on its fortieth anniversary. According to the stars, the UN is the Noah's Ark, the structure through which humankind can salvage the best it has created.

*

The UN will be the sacred shore where our drifting planet will be moored. Not Washington, not Moscow, nor any other 'capital'.

*

The UN grounds were considered a sacred place by the Manhattan Indians who called it Turtle Bay. The prophecy was that on these grounds streams of blood would flow, but that later it would be the meeting ground of all the tribes of Earth. Indeed, this is where the slaughter-houses of New York city were located and where the UN was built, born from the blood of the thirty million dead of World War II.

*

The UN is not the UN building. The UN is not even the idea which gave it birth. The UN is the manifestation of evolution wanting humanity to become one nation.

*

The fundamental problem of the human race is not the avoidance of war and the riddance of nuclear weapons. It is to find our right cosmic destiny on this planet in the universe.

*

The United Nations should not be a compromise between nations but a guiding light for humanity, the cradle of the world of tomorrow, a world seat of learning, a school of nations and heads of states.

*

We need a new vision, a new ideology for the next stage of the human journey on this planet. The UN shows us the following paths:

> Harmony with the Earth
> Harmony among all groups and peoples
> Harmony with the heavens
> Harmony with the past and the future
> Harmony of the individual with total Creation.

By its Charter, the UN is called upon to "*harmonize the actions of nations*". But it is already deeply involved in the development of these vast harmonies, far beyond the fences of nations.

*

In the UN, humanity seeks for the first time to define the universal laws which ought to rule our behavior on this planet. The United Nations Charter and the Universal Declaration of Human Rights were the first step. The Law of the Sea was the second. And there are innumerable others. As Secretary-General Perez de Cuellar pointed out, the UN has created and codified more international and world law than the entire previous human history.

*

It took more than 500 years for the ideals of the Magna Carta to permeate the western world and to culminate in the French Declaration of Human Rights and the US Declaration of Independence. It took the Oath of Strasbourg over 1000 years to become the European Community. It took the UN only forty years to become universal and to exercise momentous effects on the course of history. Just think what influence it will have over the next 500 or 1000 years! God bless the UN, this miracle of modern times, perhaps of all times.

*

The UN is a new form of evolution which should occupy the attention of the best minds of this planet. It is a comprehensive evolving network: a system of innumerable, interacting sub-systems, from nations to individuals, from the infinitely large to the infinitely small, within an ever-expanding time framework. It is an entirely new, fundamental biological phenomenon which will wipe out all former political science. We need more biologists as political leaders.

*

The crazy, incomprehensible world of today is but a giant readjustment in search of the next great step in our evolution. The UN is humanity's Holy Grail.

*

Black Elk, the Oglala Indian tells the story of the appearance of a beautiful woman-spirit, dressed in white buckskin, who predicted that a big tepee would be built in the center of the human nation. The hall of the UN General Assembly has the form of a tepee.

*

The kiwas or sacred meeting places of the Hopi Indians (the Peaceful Ones), are built in the form of domes with an opening at the center of the cupola, and right under it a hole in the ground. When a meeting takes place, a stone slab covering the hole in the ground is removed, and the elders know that they are sitting around a line which reaches from the universe to the center of the Earth. This forces them to think and deliberate with a cosmic consciousness.

The UN General Assembly Hall is built in the form of a kiwa, with an opening to the skies, but a hole remains to be dug into the ground to remind the elders of the world to think and deliberate in cosmic terms like the Hopis.

*

Humanity is one body, one brain, one heart, one soul. That is the new biology of civilization. It goes far beyond international cooperation. It encompasses each of us as the living cells of one vast human body.

*

Humanity wanders through errors and sorrows. But there is a great guiding hand behind it all. Our tribulations produce experience, experience produces hope and hope is the pathway to success. After my many years at the UN I have become convinced of the ultimate success of the human species.

*

A French professor of sociology at Vassar said in a lecture that during his youth the word international had a despicable connotation and that the League of Nations was considered as a club of lunatics.

Today, on the contrary, international relations and the United Nations have become solid, accepted realities.

*

The sum total of human wisdom and enlightenments slowly gained over the millennia will have a vastly greater impact on our future than all the arms, material wealth, and skyscrapers of today.

*

Beyond uniting nations we must become a united people. Nothing on Earth can prevent us from becoming what we want and must become for our own sake and good.

*

Our first great global chapter of history is over. We know at long last our planet and human family and their problems from every angle. The rest of this century will be devoted to the next great chapters:

> The global governance of the planet
> Its administrative management
> The new forms of human society on Earth.

*

What a world it would be if we were all bent on giving joy and happiness to others! That is the ideal offered to us by Beethoven in his "*Ode to Joy*". That is the peak of evolution we must aim at, the main purpose of the blue building of the United Nations jutting into the universe to receive God's messages of peace and happiness.

*

Positive affirmations uproot negative thoughts in us. They influence the subconscious which breeds success or failure, and shields us against external, dismal influences. This is true of individuals as it is for groups.

Therefore, if humanity repeats consistently its affirmations of peace, justice, kindness, love and brotherhood, they will become realities. This is why the UN will not fail. It is the right universal affirmative organization, miraculously born at this moment of our evolution.

*

Former Secretary-General U Thant was once asked by a journalist what he considered to be the most important event of the twentieth century. He answered:

"The birth of the United Nations on 24 October 1945."

I would even say that it was the most important event in the entire human history.

*

Far too many people and groups, especially nations, are spending their time to prove and increase their greatness instead of cooperating for the greatness of the Earth and of humanity. If God, or a team of visitors from outer space, descended on Earth, they would not be looking for the greatness of any group or person, but only for the general state of the planet and of its inhabitants. The whole world must adopt this outlook which is that of the United Nations and of its agencies.

*

The two biggest questions henceforth on this planet are:

How do we visualize our future?
How will we govern and manage our planetary home?

And almost no one on Earth devotes any attention to them. The United Nations has prepared a lot of ground on the first question, but very little on the second which seems to be taboo.

*

In the past, cultures and political identities were used to seed hatred and wage war. The UN has turned around this course and proclaimed: use your culture and identity for peace, use your power to serve, contribute your diversity to a richer world.

*

Throughout history, great wise people of all cultures have defined and proclaimed the fundamental values which should guide humans on this planet: love, truth, peace, happiness, kindness, understanding, altruism, service, cooperation, gratitude, etc. They derived their teachings from a deep understanding of the laws of the cosmos, from a mystical relation with the universe. Some considered themselves to be messengers or spokespeople of the universe or God.

Today, these same values are being affirmed, defined, advocated, promoted and progressively implemented by the first universal political organization in human history: the United Nations. This is a great momentous event in the evolution of the human race.

You therefore help the UN and the birth of a new civilization when you adopt these values in your own life and behavior and radiate them around you. You the people are the most important members and helpers of the UN.

*

"I believe without a shadow of doubt that science and peace will finally triumph over ignorance and war, and that the nations of the Earth will ultimately agree not to destroy, but to build up."

Louis Pasteur

*

A human being is something so miraculous, so well-built, so extraordinary, so incredible, that God or evolution or the cosmos must have had a reason for creating and developing us. To find that reason should be our main concern if we are to progress in our cosmic evolution.

The next great question, as so vividly evidenced by the United Nations is therefore: how are all the groups we have formed and all the institutions we have built going to help fulfill that purpose?

*

The world's relentless transformation is infinitely more important and deeper than any revolution ever conceived by humans. Revolutions are kid stuff compared with what is now going on every day. There will be no longer any revolutions on this planet, only one gigantic evolution bigger than any revolutions of the past. That is one conclusion I have drawn after four decades of observation and study of humanity at the United Nations.

*

There is no life without analysis.
There is no life without synthesis.
The United Nations is the supreme organ of both analysis and synthesis. It is a true paradigm in human evolution. But only future generations will fully understand that.

*

At the core of each human being there is a power house, a center of command, a chip of cosmic memory, a genetic bank which judges all our actions, successes and errors in trying to be fully human, i.e. to fulfill the cosmic function for which we were born on this planet in the universe.

In the end, each human being is therefore the judge of his or her own actions. Life is basically a personal story between the universe and us. At the core of humanity too there is a power house, a center of command, a cosmic memory, a genetic bank which judges all of humanity's actions, successes and errors in trying to further evolve and to fulfill the cosmic function for which humans were created on this planet in the universe.

Henceforth human evolution on this planet will be basically a story between the United Nations and the universe.

*

I once said to John Denver that in my view peacemakers and peace-institutions were marginal and powerless because evolution did not want us to go too fast.

26

He responded:

"This is no longer true. There is such an upswelling of consciousness in people all around the world today that peacemakers and peace-institutions will soon have the upper hand."

Indeed, he is right. Only individuals have life. Without them institutions are empty shells. The main agents of peace and cooperation are therefore the five billion people inhabiting this planet.

*

"I think that people want peace so much that one of these days government had better get out of their way and let them have it."

Dwight David Eisenhower, 1959

*

Introduction to a course on **Planetics** at the Institute of Political Science, Sorbonne, Paris

" The United Nations system is a unique phenomenon in human history. In 1945, after about 2 million years of existence, the human species has equipped itself with a system of management of life in all its forms on our planet. Its impact on the evolution of ideas, of research and of the application of science, of technology and of education, has not only created a new style of diplomatic relations between countries, but has also favored the emergence of a planetary culture in which the Rights of the Living are beginning to succeed the Rights of Man. The United Nations is one of the greatest human adventures since the discovery of the New World."

Claudine Brelet

*

I see the UN as the most knowledgeable, inspiring, transforming, galvanizing organization for the further evolution of humanity and of planet Earth in the cosmos.

*   *

*

2

The Manifold and Expanding Roles
of the UN

When I joined the UN in 1948 as a young man after World War
II, I was not giving the world more than twenty years before a new
world war would break out. Coming from Alsace-Lorraine where my
poor grandfather knew three wars and had five successive nationalities, where my family wore either French or German uniforms, it
seemed inconceivable to me that blacks and whites, rich and poor,
communists and capitalists, Europeans, Africans, Asians, Americans,
5000 religions, languages and innumerable minorities would ever get
along. How could they if two white, highly cultivated and educated,
advanced countries like France and Germany could not? There were
hundreds of potential seeds for a third world war on this planet. Yet,
half a century later, I am still alive and we had no world war!
Despite many conflicts and troubles, the world did not go under. In
1948, I was a very pessimistic young man. Today I am an optimistic
old man, almost sure that the human race will succeed. And this is
very largely due to the UN.

*

When I joined the UN everyone thought that the decolonization
of Asia and of Africa would take from 100 to 150 years. Yet it was
accomplished in less than forty years! Perhaps the same will be true
of other world issues, such as peace and disarmament. We usually
underestimate the will and capacity of the human race to solve its
problems. National leaders are only beginning to learn how to cope

with the new planetary challenges. They have never done it before. Given a little more time, we will successfully graduate from the present global kindergarten to a global high-school. Wars, armaments and the military will soon disappear from this planet.

*

"The UN has been a key factor in avoiding a third world war in this nuclear age. It has helped many times in damping down and often extinguishing the flames of regional and potentially global conflicts. It has achieved a generally peaceful passage of many peoples from the colonial era to independence. Nearly two-thirds of the countries that are now members of the UN attained this status through the peaceful process of decolonization.

It has codified human rights and freedoms on a global scale; it has galvanized a world response to common planetary problems: food, literacy, health, environment, resources of the sea and sea-bed, human habitat, spread of deserts, availability of water and energy, peaceful uses of space and Antarctica; and it has initiated, or forced, a dialogue between the developed and the developing nations on the question of the fair and equitable participation in the world economy.

The list is, indeed, impressive and could be lengthened.[1] The UN, although stripped of real power, has given the world more than it had the right to expect."

General Carlos Romulo
Signer of the original UN Charter

*

"Suppose that on this anniversary day the United Nations system should disappear, swallowed in the western sea that lies close at hand, what would be the results?

Children and mothers in the neediest countries would be without the major emergency and long-term assistance that makes for millions of them the difference between life and death, between productive lives and lives wasted through malnutrition and disease.

The over-all coordination of emergency aid of the drought-stricken countries of Africa would cease to the peril of the millions of

---

[1] For an illustrative list of the UN's achievements and roles, see Appendix 1.

people whose lives depend on the effective utilization of available resources.

Some ten million refugees would be without the protection and assistance now afforded by the United Nations High Commissioner for Refugees.

Multilateral negotiations on such vital disarmament objectives as the complete prohibition of chemical and of nuclear testing would stop.

Syrian and Israeli forces would be in direct confrontation on the Golan Heights with the disappearance of the peace-keeping forces positioned between them.

The presently viable channel to resolve certain key international problems, including Afghanistan, Cyprus and the Iran-Iraq war, would cease to exist.

The options available in time of crisis to prevent or restrict conflict would immediately diminish.

The list is far from comprehensive, but it is sufficient to illustrate the present importance of the United Nations to the global community."

Secretary-General
Javier Perez de Cuellar
San Francisco, 26 June 1985

*

The Useful UN

Where could the French Minister of Foreign Affairs, right in the middle of the Greenpeace crisis, meet his counterparts for New Zealand and Australia? At the UN.

Where could the US Secretary of State meet his Soviet counterpart to discuss arrangements for the forthcoming encounter between the heads of the United States and the USSR? At the UN.

Where could the representatives of Algeria and Morocco, of Greece and Turkey, of Iraq and Iran, of Israel and Arab countries, of El Salvador and Nicaragua engage into discreet conversations? Always in the famous glass building of the East River.

These encounters as well as the heads of state meetings confirm one of the most solid traditions of the UN: its corridors offer the most convenient place of encounter on the planet. Were it only for that, the child of those who signed the 1946 Charter would not have been in vain.

But there is more: by being a forum where anything can be said, the UN is a useful safety valve, especially for the powerless countries which otherwise could not be heard. We speak always of all the conflicts which have broken out on this planet. But who speaks of the conflicts which did not take place because after the voice of the delegate was heard, the voice of gunpowder was no longer necessary?

Someone pointed out that the total budget of the UN to extinguish the fires of the planet is less than that of the fire department of New York City. If someone took the pain of listing the conflicts prevented by the UN, we would see surprising results.

Yes, it has become fashionable again to be seen at the useful UN."

> *"Le Monde"*
> (Paris, 24 October 1985)

*

Who could have dreamt forty years ago ...

That an independent United Nations Commission on the Status of Women would revolutionize the laws of nationality of women, the political rights of women, discrimination against women, etc?

That an International Women's Year, a first world conference, an international Women's Day and a United Nations Decade for Women would be inaugurated in 1975?

That two further world conference would check in 1980 and in 1985 on progress or lack of progress for the world's women; that six thousand women would attend the Nairobi Conference in 1985?

That a permanent United Nations International Research and Training Institute for the Advancement of Women (**INSTRAW**) would be created?[2]

---

[2]   See appendix 2 for address of **INSTRAW**

Yes, we can proudly look back at the work accomplished by the United Nations for Women since 1945. It is one of the brightest jewels in the United Nations crown.

"We must now think of the year 2000 and plan for a world bimillennium celebration of women in that year."

INSTRAW
(October, 1985)

*

Forty Years of Building World Peace
The Caterpillar Company Salutes the United Nations

When you hear criticism of the United Nations, think for a minute what the world might be without this organization:

The dread disease of smallpox would still be ravaging human-kind. (An international campaign coordinated by the UN's World Health Organization has totally eradicated smallpox. The cost? About what the world spends on arms in three hours.)

Conflicts between Greece and Turkey, India and Pakistan, the two Koreas and other nations might have escalated to international dimensions, with the same massive destruction as in two world wars already fought this century. (UN observers and peacekeeping forces helped restore a measure of peace to these trouble spots.)

Dozens of nations - with hundreds of millions of citizens - might still be under colonial rule, with little or no ability to determine their futures. (United Nations leadership was essential in overseeing the mostly peaceful decolonization of the developing world.)

Born in the fiery dawn of the atomic age, rising from the ashes of world war, maturing in an era of tension, terrorism and uncommon peril - how could the United Nations not create impossible expecta-tions?

Yes, even after forty years of accomplishments, cynics can point to a lack of consensus in the organization, a large bureaucracy and more. But doesn't that also suggest how big and how important the UN's mission is? Getting 159 sovereign nations (the current membership) to agree on anything has never been easy, but before the UN, it had never been done.

And may be, the UN's greatest contribution is the standard it holds up to the world. For, in the words of the organization's charter, it was created "to reaffirm faith in fundamental human rights, in the dignity and worth of the human person, in the equal rights of men and women. . ." The world is a long way from attaining these goals. But they represent the highest human ideals.

Today, United Nations members represent 98 per cent of the world's people. To paraphrase words of one UN delegate, because almost everyone belongs to the United Nations, no one can afford to ignore it.

1985 marked the fortieth anniversary of the United Nations - formed in 1945 not as a world government, but as a forum "to maintain international peace and security". As such, it occupies some of the most valuable common ground in human history.

Caterpillar manufactures and distributes on a global scale, believing that the international exchange of goods and services promotes human understanding, and thus harmony and peace.

The company recognizes that the world is made up of differing races, religions, cultures, political philosophies, and economic resources. We respect those differences. Human pluralism is a strength, not a weakness.

The UN has been working to harness that strength for forty years. Caterpillar salutes the effort.

*

Captions of a Chase Manhattan Stamp Exhibit
on the Fortieth Anniversary of the UN

The Chase Manhattan Bank saluted the United Nations on its fortieth anniversary by displaying a selection of UN postage stamps, unique messengers of international goodwill. The stamps illustrated the wide scope of the United Nations' achievements and the many ways, often little known, that its work has touched our daily lives.

In a troubled world, the United Nations has sustained the age-old hope for peace:

By helping settle over 70 disputes among States.

By being the only forum to deal regularly with the great danger of world armament.

By supporting national movements that have liberated over 750 million people from foreign rule.

By sending thousands of experts and technicians to help with economic and social development.

By sending peacekeeping forces to contain tensions and conflicts in major trouble-spots.

By making human rights, for the first time in history, an international concern.

By feeding millions in times of famine and helping countries grow more food.

By improving health, fighting disease and eradicating in 1980, the ancient scourge of smallpox.

By prodding governments to deal with the problems of explosive population growth.

By immunization and feeding programs that save millions of children from death every year.

By safeguarding great treasures of art and culture.

By getting countries to report on progress in promoting the status of women world-wide.

By coordinating international efforts to fight the terrible waste of drug abuse.

By focusing global attention on the needs of millions of disabled people.

By supporting projects world-wide to engage the energy and idealism of youth.

By protecting every year, the lives and welfare of over 10 million refugees.

By creating a global consensus that we must conserve the wealth and beauty of this precious Earth.

By creating international law (more in forty years than in all previous history).

By ensuring a universal postal service and rules for safe travel by air and sea.

By negotiating treaties to make the heavens peaceful.

And getting people everywhere to think as planetary citizens, working together for a better world.

*

I consider the UN to be the birthplace of a new ethic, for it says vocally and emphatically:

No to war	Yes to peace
No to violence	Yes to cooperation
No to hatred	Yes to friendship
No to armaments	Yes to a disarmed planet
No to division	Yes to unity
No to injustice	Yes to justice
No to egotism	Yes to altruism
No to sickness	Yes to health
No to hunger and poverty	Yes to well-being
No to illiteracy	Yes to education
No to colonialism	Yes to independence
No to racism and apartheid	Yes to racial equality
No to infallibility	Yes to understanding
No to early death	Yes to longevity
No to child abuse	Yes to child love
No to slavery	Yes to freedom

No to dictatorship	Yes to democracy
No to sexism	Yes to equality of sexes
No to unemployment	Yes to a useful life
No to fanaticism	Yes to religious freedom
No to isolationism	Yes to solidarity
No to subservience	Yes to human rights
No to destruction	Yes to construction
No to pollution	Yes to a good environment
No to ugliness	Yes to beauty
No to anything that is bad on Earth	Yes to anything that is good on Earth

*

The UN system is concerned with every aspect of our place in the universe, of our planetary home, from the infinitely large to the infinitely small, and of the human family and its groupings, down to the individual person. Here is a summary of that Copernican revolution in human cooperation:[3]

Our place in the universe and our planetary home

Astroarea and outerspace	UN, UNESCO, ITU
Our relations with the sun	UN, UNESCO, FAO, WMO
The Earth's physics	UNESCO, WMO
The atmosphere	WMO, UNEP, UNESCO, ICAO

[3] See appendix 2 for the meanings of the acronyms of these UN agencies and programs. Address and telephone information is provided.

36

The Earth's climate	WMO, UNEP
Our biosphere	UNEP, UNESCO, FAO
The seas and oceans	UN, FAO, IMO, UNESCO
The polar caps	UNEP, UNESCO
The arable lands	FAO, IFAD
The deserts	UNEP, FAO, UNESCO
The mountains	UNEP, UNESCO, FAO
The Earth's water	UN, UNESCO, FAO, WMO, WHO
Plant life	UNEP, FAO
Animal life	UNEP, FAO
Human life	UN, WHO, FAO, ILO, UNESCO, IBRD
The Earth's energy	UN, UNESCO, IAEA
The Earth's crust	UN, UNESCO
The Earth's minerals	UN, UNESCO, IBRD
Microbial life and genetics	UNESCO, WHO
The world of the atom	IAEA

The Human Family

The total world population and its changes	UN, UNFPA
Human geography and migrations	UN
Human longevity	UN, WHO
Races	UN
Sexes	UN

Children	UNICEF
Youth	UN
Adults	UN and most agencies
The elderly	UN, WHO
The handicapped	UN, WHO
Our levels of nutrition	FAO, WHO
Our levels of health	WHO
Our standards of life (rich and poor)	UN, UNDP, IBRD, IMF, IFC
Our skills and employment	ILO
Our levels of education	UNESCO
Our moral levels	UN
Our spiritual levels	UNESCO
The family	UN
Human settlements	Habitat
Professions	ILO
Corporations	UN
Institutions	UN
Nations	UN and all agencies
Federations, regional organizations	UN
Religions	UNESCO
Multinational business	UN
Transnational networks	UN
World organizations	UN

The Individual

All aspects of individual life	UN (Human rights)
Good physical lives and well-being	UN, FAO, WHO
Good mental lives	UNESCO
Good moral lives	UN, UNESCO
Good spiritual lives	UNESCO

Our place in time

UNESCO is in charge of the past aspects of our planet and of our own journey in time (paleontology, archaeology, history). All UN agencies are concerned with the future of the planet and of the human species.

The above Copernican framework derived from the UN constitutes the basis for the proper management of our planetary home, and for a new political science I would call planetics.

*

I always thought that it would be fascinating to publish in one volume, all the agendas of all the UN organs and specialized agencies and world programs. It would be the most revealing encyclopedia of the world's problems and humanity's dreams and endeavors. The Union of International Associations in Brussels did it in an Encyclopedia of World Problems and Human Potentials which lists 10,233 world problems and 14,176 potentials to solve them.[4]

*

The Universal Declaration of Human Rights is one of the most noble and dignified texts ever produced by the human race. For that alone the establishment of the United Nations would have been worthwhile.

*

---

[4]   K.G. Saur - Munich, New York, Paris, London, 1986; 2nd edition 1991

Possible inscriptions for the entrance of the UN:

> Here we work for peace
> Here we defend the Earth
> Here we unite humanity
> Here we validate the individual
> Here we work for a better world.

*

"The greatest achievement of the UN is to exist."
Ambassador *Oleandrov* - USSR

*

"The existence of the United Nations is a permanent miracle."
Jean-Pierre Cot
French Minister of Cooperation

*

"The UN is not here to produce paradise but to prevent hell."
Ivor Richard
Ambassador of the UK to the UN

*

"I settle more problems and do more business in one week at the UN General Assembly in New York than in three months of travels around the world."
Henry Kissinger

*

"The UN is a constant mixture of realism and idealism."
Prince Zaddrudin Aga Khan

*

"Anyone who attacks the United Nations is a criminal because it is the most important institution on Earth. Thanks to it, we had no world war for forty years, one of the longest periods in history. I have difficulties to convince my own people because they feel let down by the UN on the Palestine question. But they must understand how vital this organization is."
Samir Shihabi
Ambassador of Saudi Arabia to the UN

*

"The basic message of the UN is love; love across nations, love across color, love across race, love across ideology, love across creed, love across cultures, love across anything."

President Kenneth Kaunda, Zambia

*

"I have seen the truth. It is not as though I had invented it with my mind. I have **seen** it, and the living image of it has filled my soul for ever ... In one day, one hour, everything could be arranged at once. **The chief thing is to love.**"

Dostoevski

*

From a speech by Douglas Roche, Ambassador of Canada for disarmament to the UN:

"In my business, I deal regularly with cynics so I know that what I am saying here will be put down as mere idealism by the self-proclaimed realists of the world, who continue to think that more weapons will bring more security. If wanting to preserve the integrity of the planet for future generations is being idealistic;

Save me from the realists who have so far produced more than 50,000 nuclear weapons with a destructive capacity one million times the power of the Hiroshima bomb.

Save me from the realists who tolerate the dire suffering of one-quarter of the world's people caught in vicious cycles of poverty as a result of the misuse of the world's resources.

Save me from the realists who think that spending $1 trillion per year on armaments - which is $2 million for every minute of every hour of every day - is buying us more security.

No, the new 'idealists' are those who think the world can go on safely piling up ever more powerful weapons systems when Nuclear Winter threatens to destroy all life on the planet. The new 'realists' are those who understand the vulnerability of the human species to nuclear destruction and want to replace the outmoded war system with a new system of collective security."

*

Napoleon introduced the concept of "absolute war". The UN and the University for Peace have introduced the concept of "absolute peace".

*

All the problems of the world, capitalism versus communism, national conflicts and hatred, the arms race, violations of human rights, overpopulation, poverty, terrorism, pollution, etc. are dumped in front of the glass house of the UN on the River of the Rising Sun, and whenever the dump truck arrives, the people inside always accept delivery. As a UN official, I sometimes feel like a world garbage collector, but humanity needs its garbage collectors too.

*

U Thant used to say that when a problem can be solved it will not reach the UN. Only insolvable problems are being brought to it.

*

Do not underestimate the role of the UN as a "talk-shop" as it is called by its detractors. One should rather call it a "talk-clinic" where national frustrations and hot feelings are often calmed down and healed by a good "talking cure". The mere role of the UN as a safety valve for national emotions in case of crisis justifies amply its existence.

*

The UN is the least expensive scapegoat nations could have invented to shift the blame and responsibility for their mismanagement of the world on someone else.

*

For Don Quixote, the UN would have been the most beloved, ideal place on Earth. Sometimes I feel like writing an autobiography under the title: *"Don Quixote at the UN"*.

*

Clausewitz, the 19th century German theoretician of war said: "War is an act of violence and there exist no limits whatever in carrying it out."

The UN says today:

"Peace is an act of love and there exist no limits whatever in carrying it out."

*

Often the task of the UN is to turn around a belief, for example, to believe in:

> Peace instead of war
> Justice instead of injustice
> A good environment instead of unbridled development
> The equality of races and of the sexes
> Non-violence as the norm of human behavior, etc.

*

The leaders of this world are not educated for a cooperative management or government of our planet. This art is being taught and developed only in the United Nations, in its specialized agencies, and in the University for Peace. I often think that all heads of states and Ministers should spend at least a year or two at the United Nations or in a specialized agency in order to learn that art.

*

The UN has become the greatest university on Earth. Its thirty-two specialized agencies and world programs are its faculties or departments.

*

From an Indonesian newspaper:

"The UN is the only world organization on which nations can pin their hope for a better future for all humankind."

How right they are! Without the UN, there would be no hope at all, no world organization whatsoever, not even a place where all leaders of nations can meet, be represented and work on an ongoing basis.

*

Statement of a woman attending a conference of the US National Council for Women:

"In all my forty years as a representative of a non-governmental organization at the UN there has never been a disagreement on the essentiality of the United Nations."

*

"In the tall glass house of the UN, members of the UN family come together and confront and articulate the world's problems and possibilities as has never been done before."

Elizabeth Cattell
NGO representative to the UN

*

"Perhaps the United Nations may be considered as a great 'all nations', 'all languages' word processor. Light or active intelligence streams into this center of humanity where world leaders and thinkers process these ideas into words through the medium of the forum of debate. The radiations of light descend vertically and at this center point of all races, they are worked out, transmitted into words and radiate forth horizontally, encircling the earth."

Brian Arrowsmith

*

Father Luis Dolan representative of the Movement for a Better World at the UN, considers UN documents to be the modern sources of Revelation, the new Scriptures. Indeed they reveal to us the universe in which we live, our right relationships with it and with each other, our good deeds and sins, our prayers, our dreams and aspirations.

I wish that someone would publish a Bible with illustrations from the United Nations. Secretary General Perez Javier de Cuellar for his part wishes that someone would publish a UN catechism for children.

*

The UN is the mediator between the "I's" of the tribes and the "We's" of the world.

*

The UN is a place where nations come to assert themselves and where in the end they adapt to each other. One could inscribe these words at the entrance of the UN:

"You who enter here, learn and go forth to serve."

*

Neither Washington, nor Moscow nor any other place on Earth will ever be the capital of the world. It is too late for that. The game is over. Nations have out smarted and out challenged each other. Only the UN has this vocation.

*

One definition of peace:
"Peace is unity ruled by law."
Empedocles

The United Nations seeks that unity but has been denied by nations the instrument of law.

*

A French aide to the Secretary-General, upon leaving the UN for a high governmental position in France, said to me:

"Never forget that you are the only people on Earth who can think and care for the world as a whole. Do not expect the President of France to do it for you. When he comes to his office in the morning, he has a coal miners' strike on his hands, or a fight in Parliament, or an election to prepare, or dozens of other worries. He does not consider it his duty to think and act for the world. That is **your** job, and you are lucky to have the time for it."

Yes, since the UN has no executive power and is not involved in the day-to-day administration of the world, it is a much more observing and reflecting place than a government. And the world badly needs a global observatory, reflecting and warning tower at this stage of our evolution.

*

According to the records kept over the years by Louis Sohn, a UN scholar, the UN was able to solve about fifty percent of all conflicts. This is not very high, but it is a good beginning. Furthermore, think what could have happened if the Cuban Missiles crisis, or the Suez crisis had not been solved.

*

Excerpts from a letter by a young American anthropologist:

"... I can share with you the general positive opinions expressed by people encountered during my travels. Most people can see through the smoke-screen of negative propaganda directed at the UN. People across the land recognize that the UN represents a great hope in promoting a peaceful future for the world. When you are effective in voicing the concerns of the oppressed, we observe a backlash by those who feel the weight of responsibility. They must either admit their transgressions or criticize the peacemakers. The political heat you are feeling, in my opinion, reflects your progress in pushing the world forward toward a better future - a process which creates friction.

Remember what the Hopi Indian elders said, 'You have power, every human being has power endowed by the Creator, spiritual power, a far more potent force.' One Hopi elder recently said after a spiritual ceremony, 'We must never stop rattling and tapping, this is one way we communicate with the Creator.' My suggestion to you and the UN is: Don't stop *rattling* the rhythms of peace, even if the UN haters dislike the music..."

Greg Schaaf

*

Isaiah said:
"They shall beat their swords into plowshares and their spears into pruning hooks: nations shall not lift up sword against nations. Neither shall they learn war anymore."

Today he might say:
"They shall beat their bombs into the United Nations and their armies into specialized agencies. Nations shall cooperate with nations and all people shall live in peace."

*

The UN often appears to me as a kind of World Mutual Life Insurance Company. One might try to conceive it in that way, reorganize it and finance it accordingly.

*

If the UN was as bad as some would like the public to believe, would more than 100 Ministers of Foreign Affairs and dozens of heads-of-state make the effort of coming each year to the UN General Assembly in New York? Certainly not.

*

The UN and its thirty-two specialized agencies and world programs are the first global attempt in human history at geo-pathology and geotherapy.

To perform its functions properly, the UN should be organized like a medical clinic:

Emergency room: (Security Council)
    urgencies
    accidents
    eruptions

Pathological sicknesses: (General Assembly)
    epidemics
    psychiatry
    convalescence and recovery
    general healing of nations and of the Earth

*

The agenda of the UN General Assembly is the yearly diagnosis of the world's troubles and hopes for healing.

*

At the UN, questions are often more important than the answers, for the questions are the first step towards enlightenment and solutions.

*

The indigenous peoples, the Africans and the United Nations have one thing in common: they feel it necessary to deliberate and to take up much time in council before an issue is resolved or a decision taken.

*

Whether existing news agencies like it or not, the UN system is already the greatest news agency on Earth and thank God, no one can buy it.

*

It is often said that nowadays knowledge is power. If this is the case, then the UN and its agencies with their knowledge of the world and of humanity are the most powerful organizations on Earth.

*

From a reader:
"The UN represents for me the pot of gold at the end of my
personal rainbow. I am absolutely certain it is about to become the
center of the great vortex of energy that will engulf the planet in its
light."

*

The UN says to the national conductors: play peace, play
justice, play better lives, play longer lives, play beauty, play happiness,
play generosity, play altruism, play friendship, play love. But many
still want to play their own discordant solos. From cacophony we
must progress to symphony.

*

The UN is a holistic organization. Those who look only at its
political activities deprive themselves of a great element of apprecia-
tion of the fundamental role it plays in shaping a better future.

*

The peace of the world requires not only the solution and
prevention of conflicts, but a whole body of managerial and administrative measures to suppress the causes of war. That side of the UN's
work is generally unknown to the public and ignored by the media.

*

In the UN building in New York, you have both the comedies
and the dramas of human destiny. The UN is both a Shakespearian
stage and a five penny opera.

*

The British Empire was built on intelligence. The UN has the
best "intelligence" (in the sense of knowledge) of the world and of its
people. It therefore is and will increasingly become the leading
agency on Earth.

*

Power nowadays is to create values in which most of the 5
billion people of this planet will believe. From that point of view the
UN is increasingly the most powerful organization on Earth. As
Napoleon said: *"Ideas are stronger than the sword."* Especially when
the sword is used to defend obsolete values.

*

The 2000-year-old Greek dream of a league of nations has been finally fulfilled by the United Nations!

*

"The current collection of thought and activity into a unified system of planetary concerns, planetary aspirations, planetary conquest over poverty, hunger, disease - planetary consciousness - aptly describes the entity of the United Nations. Teilhard de Chardin did not live long enough to see today's formidable global enterprise of the United Nations, but its stirrings into conception as the 'conscience of the world' flow from Teilhard's image of planetary consciousness."

Sister Margaret McGurn[5]

*

Napoleon wanted only the elite to be educated in order to serve him, not the people. The UN wants all the peoples of the world to be educated about our planetary home and the human family. Napoleon would not believe it, if he saw the tiny United Nations and the incredible influence it has on the world. Adolf Hitler would be totally ill.

*

The world is chaotic, but without the United Nations the world would be a complete disaster.

*

At the UN every nation or group believes to be right. Each one is usually right and performs faithfully its function. The problem is to direct all these beliefs and efforts towards what is universally right, i.e. what is right and good for humanity and for this planet, not for any particular group. This is one of the most fundamental tasks of our time and of the UN. If not, the world will remain in chaos.

*

"The UN is a gold mine, but very few nations know it or bother to pick up the gold."

Sir Robert Jackson

*

---

[5] *"Planetary Consciousness in the Thought of Teilhard de Chardin and Robert Muller"*, (World Happiness and Cooperation)

The UN is not only a cosmic but also a cosmetic business, dealing with the beauty of the world. Very often it has to repair the furrows and the scars.

*

The UN system is the world's greatest learning and teaching campus. No University on Earth can reach its stature. It is truly the world's first true, universal University.

*

Our profession at the UN is to try to heal nations and the world. Many people assume that the UN should have a 100 percent healing record. Which hospital in the world could work under such assumption?

*

The United Nations is essentially a means of communication and convergence between peoples of all cultures toward a common global social purpose: the attainment of a better world. Whether or not decisions are taken, whether or not these decisions are implemented, the United Nations slowly but surely affects its members and the people.

*

The fortieth General Assembly adopted unanimously a resolution condemning terrorism as a crime. It took 13 years from the day when, after the terrorist attack on Israeli sportsmen at the Olympic games in Munich, the Secretary-General of the UN decided to inscribe the item terrorism on the agenda of the Assembly, an unusual, unprecedented move by a Secretary-General. It paid off. His prediction was right. Every country on Earth would sooner or later suffer from terrorism.

*

I have often thought that in all UN meetings, in addition to national and delegate name-plates, there should be three more plates for spokespersons of:

The Individual   -   The Earth   -   God
*

"The UN is already a confederation of States.
The UN is perhaps the highest form of democracy."

Charles Guettel
NGO representative to the UN

*

Decolonization ... Why not speak also of deimperialization? It is one of the roles of the UN to ensure a true world democracy.

*

The defeats of the UN are defeats of humanity, not of the UN alone. My God do we wish, that there were no wars, no hatred, no violence, no injustices, no hunger, no poverty on this planet! The UN's entire efforts are aimed at that. They are the UN's daily agenda.

*

The latest and greatest explorations of the human race are outerspace, the infinitesimal small, the European community and the United Nations.

*

If you take the ideals of peace, brotherhood, understanding, justice, progress, goodwill, give-and-take, altruism, cooperation and bind them together, you will get the United Nations. It is the first institution on Earth created for the good of the entire planet and of all humanity.

*

There were very few world dreams until the UN was born. There were mostly national dreams. The UN is a hotbed of world dreams: for peace, justice, better lives, longer lives, equality of races, of sexes, human rights, a well-preserved planet, a better environment, etc. The UN is humanity's dream-house. And all its dreams will sooner or later come true.

*

In 1972, during a visit of the Secretary-General to China, Zhou En Lai expressed astonishment when Mr. Waldheim raised the question of the Middle-East, he said:

"Why discuss a problem which will still be with us in a hundred years?"

I thought that one should draw up a list of potential one-hundred-years problems and ask for their resolution.

Among the candidates would be:

> The cold war[6]
> Armaments
> Militarism
> Dictatorship
> An ungoverned world
> Violation of human rights
> The Middle-East
> The Cyprus problem
> Kashmir
> The Irish problem
>
> *

Why is it so important to prevent war? Why is the Security Council the most important organ on Earth? Because once a war has started it ends only on its own laws.

*

How many people know that the UN and some of its servers received eight Nobel Prizes, seven for peace and one for physics?

1950:	Ralph Bunche, UN mediator in the Middle East
1954 & 1981:	UN High Commissioner for Refugees
1961:	Dag Hammarskjöld Secretary General of the UN
1965:	UNICEF
1969:	The International Labor Organization
1979:	Abdus Salam of the International Atomic Energy Agency (physics)
1989:	The United Nations Peace-Keeping Forces.

*

---

[6]   Withdrawn from the list in 1989-1990, hopefully forever.

The UN is the most vast, most universal dialogue, or multilogue, ever on this planet. Socrates would be overjoyed if he saw it.

*

The things that often really matter at the UN are the invisible parts that cannot be explained.

*

Whenever there is hatred or disparagement against the UN, it is launched by people who fear its paradigmic, ethical potential which might make them lose their power. When a new door is opened in human history, there are always a good number of bad spirits who try to keep it closed.

*

Free discussion in the UN is one of its greatest merits, a gigantic learning place, an adaptive, evolutionary process towards the solution of world problems.

As Lord Macauley said:

"Men are never so likely to settle a question rightly as when they discuss it freely."

Those who criticize the UN for being a "talk-shop" are utter fools, global illiterates.

*

The world at this stage is a pressure cooker of sovereign nations, conflicts, differences in values, collisions of cultures, beliefs, group interests, etc. The UN is the safety valve of this pressure cooker. If you suppressed it, the world would explode.

*

A young UN official held that one should create a better world organization than the UN, namely a "World Organization of Happiness."

I answered that the UN was already that. Not only did it try to establish peace on Earth, the first condition to happiness, but it also dealt with the health, education, nutrition and basic human needs and rights of the people. The ultimate objective of the UN and of its specialized agencies is indeed "the pursuit of happiness" for all humans.

*

What would we think today of the people who at the birth of the US Federal Government under George Washington did nothing but criticize his efforts under the pretext of bureaucracy? Basically they were against the creation of the United States. Or of the people who in the 1930's were harping at the expenses of the League of Nations when Hitler, Mussolini and the Japanese were about to give a death blow to that first international organization? Why do some people continue to play this damaging game against the UN? Will they never grow up?

*

The moral law is the law that lifts. That is the real strength of the UN.

The UN is the Agora of the world. And the Agora was often a very unruly place.

*

The role of the UN is to transform a mess into a mesh.

*

A desert proverb quoted by an Algerian delegate in response to criticisms against the UN:

"Do not throw away any water before you have found fresh water."

*

We need yearly balance-sheets of what is improving and what is deteriorating on this planet.

Improvements are:
- Our knowledge of our planet and of our place in the universe;
- Increasing peace, welfare, health, cooperation, and spirit of life;
- Our diminishing wars, epidemics, misunderstandings, conflicts and hatred.

Deteriorating are:
- Drug addictions, alcoholism, morality, the family;
- The immune system of the human body;
- Our ecosphere, nature, our forests, our fellow species.

The UN and its 32 agencies and world programs are all involved in establishing such yearly balance-sheets, or states of the world. But very few people know it. Most children are never taught about them in school. The media seldom report on them.

*

Peace is not the ultimate objective. It is only a condition for the fulfillment of the divine gift of life, a precondition to human happiness.

The United Nations therefore, is not the ultimate objective. It is only an instrument, a relay for peace, for a better management of planet Earth, and for the happiness and fulfillment of all humans admitted to the miracle of life.

*

When I finished my first book, *"Most of All They Taught Me Happiness"*, my wife expressed surprise: "After so many years at the United Nations, all you produce is a book on happiness? Couldn't you write a book on the UN?"

I answered: "The objective of life is happiness. To enjoy happiness we must have peace. The United Nations is a major instrument for peace. Hence, my love and devotion to the United Nations, but only as an instrument of happiness. You will find that my book is in a large degree a book on the United Nations."

*

The UN is the weakest political organization ever devised by the human mind. It has no legislative, executive, judicial or taxing power, and no sovereignty. It cannot even secure a loan! Yet, it is expected to perform miracles of which it has performed quite a few. People often question the efficiency of the UN. I am personally amazed at its efficiency, given the circumstances.

*

People must be joking. How do they expect the United Nations to ensure peace on Earth when the UN is given 800 million dollars a year to solve every problem under the sun including world peace, yet the military are given one thousand billion dollars a year to build up their dreadful armaments? Visitors from other planets would consider us the most insane, irrational species in the universe. They would immediately reverse the figures.

*

After a speech I delivered to the Chief State School Officers of the US on the subject, 'Education for a World Perspective', the Chairman of the meeting commented:

"We are concerned with American education in a world perspective. Today we heard a planetary citizen who spoke to us about education from a world perspective, a right education for all humanity, for the good of our world and for the evolution of the entire human race."

I was happy that he had understood me so well.

*

The UN reminds me of the story of two gypsies walking together when it started to rain. One had an umbrella; he opened it but it was full of holes and his friend asked:
"Why did you take along an umbrella full of holes?"
Second gypsy: "I didn't think that it would rain."

In the case of a serious world crisis, nations might discover that the UN is an umbrella full of holes, and they did not find it necessary to patch the holes when there was time.

*

Beware: Those who criticize the UN do not want a better UN, they want to destroy it so that they can benefit from the present world chaos and better exploit it for their personal profit.

*

Many people, when judging the UN, forget that it is an organization of independent, sovereign states. It is not a world government. It cannot legislate. It is only a place where member states meet to try to resolve conflicts, to discuss mutual concerns and to use international machinery to cooperate and to resolve common problems. The UN is and can only be as strong as the collective will of its members.

*

You don't throw stones at a cathedral because people continue to sin.

You don't throw stones at a hospital because it does not heal every patient.

You don't throw stones at the UN because it does not solve every conflict and problem of the world. People who do are foolish.

*

Someday governments will bitterly regret not having supported and strengthened the United Nations to the satisfaction of evolution. They could have survived much longer with a strong United Nations as their global instrument. The weaknesses of the UN will dig their graves.

*

The goal of the United Nations is human harmony. And goodwill is the principal means to achieve harmony.

*

Humanity has eradicated smallpox from this planet thanks to the World Health Organization. We must also eradicate bigpox, namely armaments, especially nuclear armaments. We will succeed in that eradication too and reap huge benefits.

*

The UN is the weakest and most influential institution on Earth. Even if the Charter is broken, even if there continue to be conflicts, even if member nations misbehave, the UN must be maintained as a school and playground for the unruly children states who have begun their education in global and cosmic behavior.

*

The world needs a new high position, that of a 'Great Reconciliator' who would reconcile all nations and large entities. In a way, the Secretary-General of the United Nations is a World Reconciliator.

*

It is with the United Nations Charter as it is with abstinence: One can not break it a little bit, one breaks it, period. Governments all too often forget this.

*

The UN is a school of democracy for the new, young nations. We must be patient with them. The older nations were not better in their early age, and often are not even better today, to say the least.

*

We must keep our life clean of the impurities of current social turmoil and political strife. If not, we will lose sight of the real, deep purpose of the miracle given to us by God. The world society and politics will still remain deleterious for some time. Therefore, protect yourself by being yourself in order to remain yourself.

The same is true of the United Nations. We must see its deep fundamental meaning and purpose, not the political impurities with which it is fraught. Those are merely unclean birth materials.

*

The UN is a temperature gauge of the world.
When there is a cold war, the entire UN diplomacy freezes.

*

At the Frankfurt Bookfair I learned that the United Nations and its agencies are the biggest publisher on Earth in terms of subjects and titles. This reflects the vast scope of the UN's planetary work.

*

"The grim fact is that we prepare for war like precocious giants and peace like retarded pygmies."

Lester Pearson
former Prime Minister of Canada

*

U Thant used to say:
"When I am equally criticized by the US and the USSR, I know that I am right."

*

I once said to U Thant during the 25th anniversary of the UN:
"Why don't you recommend that the UN be closed? Then at least the hypocrisy and irresponsibility of nations will be glaring."

He answered sadly: "It would not help much. They would meet almost immediately to create another United Nations, probably weaker than the present one."

*

The UN is the greatest service organization on Earth. Its officials are rightly called world servants. This is why all the great service organizations (Rotary, Lions, Jaycees, etc.) are represented at the UN as NGOs.

*

Whenever I hear or read of UN inefficiency, bureaucracy, lack of coordination, duplication and excessive expense, I open a new file, for it means that an anti-UN policy has been decided somewhere. The public invariably is misled, and falls into its trap.

*

Father Griffiths, who represented a Catholic organization at the UN, used to explain the usefulness of the UN as follows:

Two peasants are working in the field when a jet airplane overflies them at a very high altitude.

First peasant: "I would hate to be up there in such a machine."

Second peasant: "I would hate it even more to be up there without one."

For Father Griffiths, the same was true of the UN.

*

When the ballot box of the UN Security Council was opened for the first time in 1946, it contained the following note:

"May I who had the privilege of fabricating this ballot box, cast the first vote. May God be with every member of the UN Organization, and through your noble efforts bring lasting peace to us all, all over the world."

Signed: *Paul Antonio*, mechanic

These words should be inscribed in golden letters on that ballot box and be read by delegates before casting their votes.

*   *
*

3

The UN and its Member-Governments

The following words of British and French statesmen on the day of demise of the League of Nations still apply to the attitude of many member-states towards the United Nations today:

"Why then, did it fail? Its failure was not due to any weakness in the terms of the Covenant. To my mind it is plain beyond the possibility of doubt that it failed solely because the Member States did not genuinely accept the obligation to use and support its provisions. That was due to several causes. Speaking of my country, I must admit that the general current of official opinion was either neutral or hostile. I suspect that was also true in other countries. There were other causes, but that alone was enough to prevent success. It was not so much that the principles of the League were rejected. Few people hated it. Most people desired peace but governments seemed to think that all they need do was to give a general and somewhat tepid approval to its work and, if that was not enough, it did not matter. Inter-war opinion greatly underrated both the danger of the international situation and the difficulty of applying efficient remedies."

Lord Cecil
the United Kingdom

"It is not the League which has failed. It is not the principles which have been found wanting. It is the nations which have neglected it. It is the Governments which have abandoned it. The League of Nations was not a deceit. It lived vividly in the heart and spirit of countless multitudes. It labored. It leaves behind it lasting works. Some fully succeeded and the UN will merely have to carry them on. This applies to its efforts in the field of intellectual cooperation, public health, transit, social questions and rural life. It was closely associated with the work of Nansen on behalf of refugees. It took a leading part in those great migrations between Greece and Turkey which took place in all directions. Finally, it played a decisive role in the financial and monetary reconstruction of countries ravaged by the first world war. It succeeded as long as Governments, and particularly the governments of the great powers, put their faith in it and animated and fortified it by their will and as long as the possibility could always be more or less perceived in the background that their force would be put at the service of its decisions.

If I draw this somber picture, it is not to engage in vain recrimination over the past, still less to make my mea culpa at the cost of others. I do not forget that certain French Governments had their share of backsliding. It is, on the contrary, to emphasize my hope that the recognition of these errors and the determination to repair them which finds expression in the Charter of the United Nations will in the future preserve us from such mistakes."

Mr. Paul Boncour
France

*

U Thant was once asked by a journalist, "What is in your view the greatest obstacle to peace?"

He answered:

"The policy my nation, right or wrong."

He could have added:

"My religion, right or wrong"
"My ideology, right or wrong"
"My company, right or wrong," etc.

*

"Does it behove the powerful to put a brake even on the slow progress towards evolution of an order? How will it profit them to abort the hope and the faith that the United Nations system symbolizes?

The biggest threat to humankind posed by the division of the world into rival military blocs is a negation of the philosophical vision of the United Nations Charter whose essence is peaceful coexistence."

Rajiv Gandhi

*

From an interview with Ambassador Aba Eban, of Israel:
Question:
"In view of your negative comments on international organizations, and especially in view of the fact that Israel has been vilified over the last several decades, why do you think Israel should continue its membership in the United Nations?"

Answer:
"What I said about the United Nations is that claims of its being a panacea for the world's ills were exaggerated and that the organization has fallen victim to unnecessary disillusion. But let there be no misunderstanding. One of its virtues, or qualities, is that it does define the international system. It does by membership award the identity of a nation, and membership in the United Nations is still the only valid and widely accepted credential for nationhood. Therefore, for a country to surrender those credentials - especially for us, the only country that has fought for them - because we hear some harsh words, I think would be folly.

I would even recommend to a great power such as the United States not to carry its rancor sometimes to the point of wanting to leave. It is possible to hear unpleasant things about oneself without tearing up one's own identity card. That is what I recommend for us and for others."

In other words, if the United Nations were to disappear, the international recognition of Israel as a State would be in serious jeopardy.

*

Compared with the growth of world problems, of big business and of national governments, the UN's relative position diminishes every year due to the shortsightedness of its members. This will lead in the end to the death of the nation-state system which did not seize the UN as an opportunity to manage and govern this planet properly.

*

The nation system of this planet resembles its sport system: the peoples take sides and want "their" team to win. It is like the Olympics or the World Soccer Games, but there is one difference. International sports have strict rules of behavior, the violation of which may mean the expulsion of a player or team. There is nothing like that in the UN. Any member can break the rules of the game and continue to play. The bigger they are, the rougher and tougher they play. They often even refuse to pay their dues and are not expelled!

*

Nations have the immense privilege of having their national sovereignty recognized by the UN. Several of them even owe their existence to the UN. The least one could expect from them is to honor faithfully their obligations under the Charter. Any agreement implies give and take. You cannot expect only to take and never to give. The future of the nation system depends on that.

*

At the United Nations, the big powers should shoulder the biggest responsibilities, and the powerless poor countries should have the biggest rights. This is how history has always progressed towards greater justice. But the big powers are engaged in a vast effort to make their people believe exactly the contrary. In the long run this might mean their demise.

*

The greatest contribution of the UN to Panama, according to its former President, Jorge Illueca, was not economic and technical assistance. It was the holding of the Security Council in Panama City, which helped his country to resolve its problems with the United States regarding a new treaty for the Panama Canal. Each country, during the fortieth anniversary of the UN, stressed a special meaning or service rendered to it by the UN. Several countries owe their independence to the UN and have made 24 October, UN Day, their national holiday.

*

A UN maxim:

When there is a problem between two little countries, the problem disappears. When there is a problem between a big country and a little one, the little country disappears. When there is a problem between the two big powers, the UN disappears. And when there is agreement between the two big countries, the UN disappears too.

*

"There is nothing wrong with the United Nations, except its governments."

Lord Caradon
Representative of the UK to the UN

*

Can anyone imagine what the UN would be if the big powers decided to make it work and financed it properly? It cannot be repeated enough that the failures of the UN are mainly attributable to the big powers.

*

The big powers are merely doing what all powers have done throughout history. They turn to the weak and say:

"We will protect you, but you must align with us".

The Romans did it, the feudalists did it, the colonialists did it. Because of this they will fight tooth and nail the establishment of a world security system. Disarmament presupposes security. Security presupposes a reduction in power. The power contest among nations therefore remains the root cause of world insecurity and armaments.

*

It is hard to understand why the United States, which has on its soil the most unique cradle of a new world vision and order, is not using the UN to guide the world and to pursue its dream on a planetary level.

*

There is always talk of the poor image of the UN. But no one ever speaks of the poor images of the big powers who are the real culprits of the world chaos, not the poor, powerless UN.

*

Humanity grows and so do its problems. They are all brought to the UN. But in the eyes of the big powers, the UN is not supposed to grow. Nearly every year they ask for its "freeze". The shrinking effectiveness of the UN is therefore not the fault of the UN, but that of the big powers.

*

The UN Charter, originally drafted by the United States is basically a western, Christian inspired text. Not a single sentence in it can be construed to be of communist inspiration. And yet, the United States seems to have abandoned this wonderful, democratic instrument and platform designed to guide the world towards a better, just, peaceful and prosperous order. Historians will find this hard to understand. What a golden opportunity and truly historic challenge the US is missing.

If the US does not wake up to the need for leadership in a UN it has created, I am afraid the US will be overtaken by the world.

*

The UN is an organization of the sheep for the sheep but with a few big wolves in it.

*

I found this text stamped on an envelope:
"Please discount the political rhetoric and have faith in the United Nations and in America."

*

The United Nations should have precedence over every nation.

*

Many countries with different cultures, customs, beliefs, languages, systems of government live peacefully side by side despite their differences. However other countries find it impossible to follow this good example. So one must point the finger at them as being the main culprits for the present unrest and armaments insanity in the world.

*

The best peace organization is useless if it is not used.

*

The powerful groups and power candidates who share among themselves the fate of the world know instinctively that the UN will be the ultimate way. Scared by this prospect, they damage and retard the inevitable course by weakening, denigrating and financially strangulating the world organization. They in turn program their people with indifference or hostile feelings towards it.

*

The world by now should already be in good order and in peace. Why do nations procrastinate? Why don't they hurry up, so that we can turn to much more vital tasks than the present antiquated, time and resource consuming quarrels?

*

The US should be extemely happy to have the United Nations located on its soil:

-      It pays only one quarter of its budget and gets in return three times more income;

-      It has become the main center of world diplomacy, replacing Europe in this role;

-      It offers the US a primary role in establishing a proper world order;

-      It gets world-wide media attention and coverage of UN meetings (Security Council, yearly General Assembly, visits and meetings of heads of states, etc.);

-      It has better control, influence and possibilities to put pressure on the world organization;

And yet one seldom hears a word of praise or thanks from the US, but many complaints.

*

There are dozens of countries in the world who would lick their fingers and be proud to be the seat of the UN.

Someday it might happen. History will then write that after the failure of Europe (demise of the League of Nations) and of the United States, the effort at world organization moved to another continent.

*

The UN is writing the history of our contemporary world. It is a reflection, a giant mirror of the behavior and misbehavior of nations.

*

The leaders of the US and of the USSR for a long time were voluntary excommunicates: they did not want to communicate with each other.[7] In the meantime others nations, through communications in the UN and in its specialized agencies, gave birth to another ideology, to a new vision of the world.

*

Political tensions and instability are detrimental to all nations, including the big ones.

*

The United Nations is seen as a danger by the big powers, because it is breeding a new ideology which will make the prevailing ones obsolete.

*

Do not blame the electrical system if the switch is not on or a fuse is blown. Put the switch on or replace the fuse.

This is true also of the UN: for many years the main switch, namely cooperation between the US and USSR was not on. Once the switch was on the UN worked, because this is how the system was designed.

*

In San Francisco the US State Department has personnel entrusted with the reception of about 3000 foreign dignitaries invited each year by the United States to visit that city.

I was thinking: why is it, the US does not invite one foreign dignitary instead of all those 3000, namely the president of the USSR? Would the anniversary of the signature of the UN Charter not be a

---

[7]   1991: Thank God, this has changed and the UN has greatly benefitted.

magnificent occasion to do that, as I have repeated during the past year? [8]

If anyone had invited Adolf Hitler to visit the vast Soviet Union and the immense United States, it is probable that there would not have been any World War II. Its 30 million dead, victims of the holocaust and hundreds of billions of material losses could have been avoided with a little money spent on two simple trips. But simplicity and common sense are rare in politics.

*

The UN reminds me of the Arab proverb:

"You can take the camels to the water, but you cannot make them drink."

You can take governments to the conference table, but you cannot make them act.

*

Nations should use the UN as the principal forum to express their values, ideals and ideas for the improvement of human destiny and the fate of the Earth. To complain about others is a waste of time.

*

Former Secretary-General U Thant once remarked that there were no longer any foreign affairs of nations. Such affairs are now the internal affairs of the world, and world affairs have become the internal affairs of nations. Ted Turner, founder of CNN, for his part fines any of his employees who use the words *foreign affairs* the sum of one hundred dollars. It is also time to rename Ministries of Foreign Affairs - Ministries for Peace or Ministries of World Affairs or Ministries of World Cooperation. Which nation will be the first to do it?

Even better, given the importance and impact of world affairs, I recommend that each country should have a President for the

---

[8] Presidents Reagan and Gorbachev finally met for the first time during the fortieth anniversary of the UN, in Geneva. It was a turning point in US/USSR relations and in the recent history of the world.

68

country's affairs and a Co-President for world affairs, (or vice-versa) the two working intimately together on a daily basis in the same office.

*

The UN Charter is an integral part of US Law. It is published in the Statutes of US Law and was ratified by the US Congress. When the President of the US takes his oath of office, he swears to uphold US law, including the UN Charter. This is why the original copy of the Charter is deposited with the US government in Washington. The US has a sacred duty to uphold it.

*

The US has little patience and perseverance. Having had the vision of the United Nations, after a short forty years it seems to give up on it. Does this mean that a fundamental American dream is waning? Or does it mean that like with President Wilson's idea of a League of Nations in 1918, a small but powerful minority is trying to destroy that dream? [9]

*

It was quite a sight to see Prime Ministers Rajiv Gandhi of India and Zia Ul Haq of Pakistan walk arm in arm, smiling at each other, cheerful and young, into the dining room of the Secretary General for the fortieth anniversary dinner. They had met only twice before, at what I call the "funeral diplomacy", namely at the funerals of Mr. Chernenko and of Mrs. Gandhi. I believe much goodwill can come out of the talks between the two men.

Indeed, thanks to the good relations established during the heads of states meeting at the UN, the leaders of seven South Asian countries (Bangla-Desh, India, Sri Lanka, Bhutan, Nepal, Maldives

---

[9] The newspaper "*Le Monde Diplomatique*" in Paris devoted one third of its special issue on the fortieth anniversary of the UN, (24 October, 1985), to the international campaign waged by the US isolationists against the UN. It pointed out that the campaign for the withdrawal of the US from UNESCO was the first step of this overall objective.

and Pakistan) decided to establish a South Asian Association of Regional Cooperation and to meet regularly at the head of state level.

*

From the speech of an African delegate:
"It is not the UN that has not kept pace with the expectations of the US. It is the US vision, idealism and commitment which has not kept pace with the advances of the UN."
This could be said of many nations. Each member state should examine its conscience in this respect.

*

There are no big countries and little countries. There are no powerful and powerless countries. There are no rich countries and poor countries. There is only one Earth of which we are all part, one universe of which we are living, breathing cells. If you discover that, you will see the truth everywhere, you can no longer be fooled by anyone.

*

The type of news we get at the UN from member governments:
"The US Congress voted today to install twenty-one more MX missiles in order to facilitate disarmament."

*

Most hypocritical of all are the big powers who established the UN and now harass, stifle and criticize it relentlessly, when in reality they are the main culprits of its malfunctioning and of the mess in the world. Perhaps they resort to that constant criticism in order to hide their own capital sins and culpability. For them the UN is a convenient scapegoat.

*

In 1970, on the 25th anniversary of the UN, the US Congress established a Committee to evaluate the UN after 25 years. Hearings were held in major cities and with many peoples' organizations. In 1985, while most nations of the world engaged into such evaluations on the fortieth anniversary, the US did not bother. An objective evaluation of the UN is still due to the American people. The cheap anti-UN slogans spread around by vocal isolationists are undignified

and unworthy of the American people. They must be corrected and
brought into true democratic perspective.

*

With the United Nations, the world is a disorderly mess of
nations, but without the United Nations it would be a total chaos.
Numerous are those who criticize the United Nations, but too few
voice better to proposals. Let us all speak up.

*

"This is a world of unlimited possibilities and a world of
unlimited disasters."

Sir Brian Urquhart

*

My wife, who was a delegate of Chile to the UN General
Assembly and to the Security Council, once came back from a session
of the World Health organization in Geneva and had this comment:
"Why don't the politicians in the General Assembly follow the good
example of the Ministers of Health: instead of accusing each other,
they simply report on the health situation of their country, on what
they tried, where they failed, where they succeeded, and they make
practical proposals for international action by the WHO."
Indeed, what a different UN General Assembly it would be if all
heads of states, Ministers of Foreign Affairs and Ambassadors did the
same and made the General Assembly the assembly of good health
and peace of the planet.

*

Humanity devotes incalculable resources to improve technology,
to have better cars, better planes, better trains, etc. But should we
not devote also at least a little attention to the improvement of our
planet's political system? We don't. The trickle of resources put into
the UN and its agencies is a crass example of that neglect. Our
current political leaders should be ashamed of their lack of world
vision. Someday historians will call them dwarfs at the onset of the
global age. Very few will be remembered in the next century.

*

Franklin Roosevelt wanted the UN to be established in San
Francisco so that European delegates who in 1945 had to travel by

boat to New York and to cross the US by train, would see the vastness of the US and realize the stupidity of wars between the tiny European nations.

Today the heads of states, especially those of the big powers, should be put in space capsules to circle the Earth to fully realize their cosmic responsibilities and come up with a new political system for the planet.

*

Doesn't the sophisticated, incomprehensible arms debate between the two big powers remind us of the sophisticated, incomprehensible legal debate at the end of the Roman Empire? Rather than signs of greatness and power, they are signs of decadence, of the dissolution of a wrong political system, of a misreading of evolutionary trends. I would like to be a historian in the third millennium to see how this will end and how it will be judged in retrospect.

*

The golden rule at the UN should be:

No complaints, only ideas, concrete proposals and actions.

If I were the Secretary-General I would get up and leave the Assembly Hall each time a delegate accuses another country, and return only when ideas, proposals and positive statements are made. Delegates should do the same.

*

If a commission of experts from outer-space visited our earth, they would note that this world is profoundly divided between two giant atomic powers who have cast their division and hostility into the most sophisticated art ever conceived.

They would further conclude that the efforts of the non-aligned countries will not be able to change this situation, and that a better world would only ensue from a reconciliation between the two giants. They would recommend such reconciliation as the priority item on the agenda of world affairs.[10]

*

---

[10] Written in 1984. Thank God it has happened since then.

The people lament the conflicts still prevailing on Earth. Would it not also be good to remember the vast number of nations who live in peace with each other, and thank them?

*

Despite all the human troubles, errors and governmental idiocies I witnessed in the United Nations during four decades, I am more convinced than ever that humanity will succeed.

*

The United States is a member of the United Nations.
The United Nations is not a member of the United States.
And this is true of every other country on Earth.

*

"We have created a one world before we were ready for it."

Dag Hammarskjöld

Well, we better step up our readiness for it.

*

Any war is a violation of the principles of the UN Charter which calls for the peaceful settlement of disputes. With the adoption of the UN Charter, there are no longer any just wars.

*

Critics say that the expectations placed in the UN after World War II were too high. In my view, the expectations placed in the UN can never be too high. It is the ideals, goals, dreams and policies of governments which have remained too low.

*

Roosevelt was a genius to get the United Nations established in the United States, and other continents were fools to let it go.

If the UN should ever fail or if the US should give it up, it would be the turn of Asia, Latin America or Africa to have the next try at world order on this planet. Why not Costa Rica, a jewel of a country, totally disarmed and demilitarized by Constitution, a model of democracy, of human rights, of natural beauty and conservation, the country on Earth which comes closest to UN ideals. It would deserve to be the seat of the world organization.

*

One should not have any illusions about the attitudes of the big powers towards the United Nations. They were never really in favor of a strong, effective world organization. Their veto attitude which started right from the beginning has never ceased and is aggravated today by a **de facto** financial veto. They are smothering the organization at the precise moment when the planet needs infinitely more world cooperation. Even with the end of the cold war, when one should expect an immense strengthening of the UN, there is only talk of cost reduction, budgeting cuts, etc. Future historians will judge today's leaders harshly. They were dwarfs on the eve of a gigantic planetary era.

*

Governments are dividing the world like football teams. Each wants to mark points over the other, and the people watch the games like fans, rejoicing at the points marked by their team. As long as the people will enjoy these games, there will be little chance for peace in the world. The first step, therefore, is for every person on Earth to despise and ignore those political games and competitions. Without applause and support, the captains of the teams will give up their games and mind their real business.

*

In 1971, when visiting the UN, astronaut Alan Shephard said to Secretary-General U Thant:
"If everyone could see the Earth from the moon, as we saw it, all the problems before the UN would be solved."
Decades later, none of the leaders of the Earth nations have as yet adopted this point of view. What they lack most is a lunar, solar, cosmic, or universal outlook.

*

Most heads of states condemn terrorism and violence, but at the same time they do not mind delivering speeches full of violence, hatred and incitement to violence.
They remind me of a remark by U Thant:

74

"Dear Robert, you westerners have only discovered physical violence but you ignore the fact that physical violence is preceded by verbal violence. Western speeches, writings and media are full of violence, and this is not considered abnormal. And above all, you have not discovered the origin of all violence: the violence in the mind, mental violence."[11]

*

War is the most extreme, most despicable form of violence, for it clothes itself with glory, heroism, medals, monuments, uniforms, memorials and the whole battery of pseudo-ethics invented by power-drunk nations.

*

This planet has too much internal strife, for wars between nations are not external troubles but internal strifes of the human species. This planet is too small to be divided into 179 corrals.

*

An ideal head of state should give these simple instructions to his or her delegation to the UN:
Defend and illustrate what we believe.
Learn from what others believe.

*

Costa Rica can proudly report to the world that it has gone further than any nation in implementing the request of the UN Charter for non-recourse to violence: it has purely and simply outlawed the military by Constitution in 1949 and has lived in peace ever since, the only peaceful country in Central America. Which nation will follow its good example and become the second country on the demilitarized, disarmed honor list of this planet?

*

---

[11]   It is in remembrance of this statement that in June 1992, during the UNCED II conference in Rio de Janeiro, Sushil Kumar the spiritual leader of the 20 million Jains and I decided to launch a World Movement of Non-Violence for peace and the environment.

At none of its anniversaries should the UN have to apologize. On the contrary, it is member governments which must apologize for their mistakes, arrogance and misbehavior, not the UN. At each anniversary of the UN member governments must recommit.

*

After watching them for thirty-eight years in the United Nations, I can only say that the policies of the United States and of the USSR are a major biological aberration. Except for Franklin Roosevelt, none of their leaders will go down in history with an everlasting image. They might have been meritorious of their people and of their systems, but none of them earned the gratitude and applause of the world. In the great new global age of humanity, they will be soon forgotten.

*

Since the main reason for the malfunctioning of the UN is the cold war, the rest of the nations should give the US and USSR an ultimatum to work together. If they don't, the world organization should be moved to a third world continent.[12] Forty years of obstructing the good functioning of the UN is enough. Moreover, the UN is too precious to be kept in a first-risk atomic fall-out zone like the United States.

*

A Japanese colleague of mine had this to say after a year at the United Nations:
"When I was in Japan, I was convinced, as are all my colleagues in Foreign Affairs, that the UN is dominated by the third world countries. Now I discover to my amazement that they have little if any power. In thousands of open or subtle ways the UN is still by and large dominated by the big powers."

*

One of the most unfair yearly reports by the US State Department is on how UN member countries voted "against the US". In the first place, no one can vote against the US, because the US seldom

---

[12] With the end of the cold war, things have fortunately changed.

puts up any proposals in the UN. Secondly, countries vote on issues not against countries. If African countries vote against the policies of the South African government and the US supports South Africa, that cannot be construed (but alas is) as a vote against the US! Thirdly, it is really outrageous to exclude from such statistics decisions taken by consensus, which constitute the largest number of actions by the UN at the request of the big powers. Also, by what aberration are countries who abstain or are absent counted as having voted "against the US"? More appropriate would be a yearly report listing how the US voted against the UN!

*

We have eradicated many diseases on this planet, but we have not yet eradicated the worst of them: excessive, world-irresponsible, disrespectful, unnatural, arrogant national sovereignty.

*

In the home of an Austrian family, I saw an engraving showing the encounter between Czar Alexander of Russia, King Friedrich Wilhelm of Prussia and Emperor Franz I of Austria. They were shaking hands with each other and the picture had this caption:

"*Sie einten sich wie Brüder, Europa athmet wieder.*"
("They united as Brothers, Europe breathes again.")

In my mind I visualized the picture of the heads of state of the US and USSR meeting and shaking hands, with the caption:

"*Sie trafen sich wie Menschen, die Welt athmet wieder.*"
("They met as Human Beings, the World breathes again.")[13]

*　*
*

---

[13] Thank God they did.

4

The UN's World Servants

Pope John Paul II said to UN officials during his historic visit to the United Nations in 1979:

"You are the carvers of the stones.

The builders of the pyramids in Egypt and Mexico, of the temples in Asia, of the cathedrals in Europe were not only the architects who laid out the designs, or those who provided financing, but also, and in no small way, the carvers of the stones, many of whom never had the satisfaction of contemplating in its entirety the beauty of the masterpiece that their hands helped create. And yet, they were producing a work of art that would be the object of admiration for generations to come.

You are in so many ways the carvers of the stones. Even a lifetime of dedicated service will not always enable you to see the finished monument of universal peace, of fraternal collaboration and of true harmony between peoples. Sometimes you will catch a glimpse of it, in a particularly successful achievement, in a problem solved, in the smile of a happy and healthy child, in a conflict avoided, in a reconciliation of minds and hearts achieved. More often, you will experience only the monotony of your daily labors, or the frustrations of bureaucratic entanglements. But know that your work is great and that history will judge your achievements with favor.

The challenges that the world community will face in the coming years and decades will not diminish. The rapidly changing pace of world events, the tremendous steps forward of science and technology will increase both the potential for development and the complexity of the problems. Be prepared, be capable, but above all have confidence in the ideal you serve."

*

"Gods vision is executed in and through the most dedicated servers and lovers of the United Nations.

There are a few, very few, supremely dedicated servers and lovers of the United Nations who are the harbingers of the supreme glory that the United Nations embodies. They will always remain in the vanguard of the supreme vision that the United Nations is offering and forever will offer throughout the length and breadth of the world. What the United Nations has in the inner world is peace, boundless peace, and what it has within is bound to come to the fore in the near and distant future to inundate the outer world."

> *Sri Chinmoy*
> Director - UN Meditation Group

*

Once during a meeting, Secretary-General Perez de Cuellar scribbled this note which he gave me:

"There is no more beautiful profession on Earth than to unite humans."

*

Received from a reader:
"The vision and purpose of the UN can be portrayed in a very human way by focussing on the lives of UN leaders, on events during their tenures. Just as the life of Mahatma Gandhi reveals in a microcosm the history of India and a personal commitment to the people of his nation, the lives of various Secretaries-General can reveal the story and meaning of the United Nations and their commitment to all peoples as one family."

*

In the new independent India, Mahatma Gandhi used to instruct government officials that whenever they were faced with a difficult decision, they should remember the face of the poorest human being they had ever seen, and ask themselves whether their decision would benefit that poor person or not. The same image should guide UN officials. I keep in my office the shattered helmet of a dead soldier from World War II, to remind me why I am here.

*

The participation of the UN staff in the commemoration of the fortieth anniversary of the UN took three forms:

Recognition: All staff members with more than thirty years of service received scrolls signed and handed by the Secretary-General in a general meeting of the staff in the Assembly Hall;

Rededication: All staff members were asked to renew solemnly their oath of office;

Reflection: The staff organized discussion groups and seminars on the UN's objectives, work and idealism.

*

The UN oath of service:

"I solemnly swear to exercise in all loyalty, discretion and conscience the functions entrusted to me as an international civil servant of the United Nations, to discharge these functions and regulate my conduct with the interest of the United Nations only in view, and not seek or accept instructions in regard to the performance of my duties from any Government or other authority external to the Organization."

*

In my view, there is not a single person on Earth who has the qualities required of a Secretary General of the United Nations. There are schools for everything on this planet except for world servants and heads of states. Yet, the UN must become the most noble world association of virtuous men and women ever seen on this planet.

If there is a need for the most knowledgeable, most understanding, most idealistic, most loving, most visionary and most spiritual people on Earth, it is at this vortex of the world: the United Nations.

*

The jobs of Alexander the Great, Caesar and Napoleon were insignificant compared with that of the Secretary-General of the UN. They were wrong jobs anyway.

*

"As far as the nature of the Secretary General's personality is concerned, I feel that he or she should be the kind of man or woman who looks to the future, a futurist, and has a global conception of problems. I do not believe in the importance of regional considerations in the choice of a Secretary General. I do not believe that only an Asian or an African or a Latin American or a European should be the next Secretary General. What I believe in are the qualities of the head as well as of the heart, like moral integrity, competence, and the ability to· project into the future, to act within the framework of a global unit, and a genuine desire to see this organization develop into a really effective instrument for peace, justice, and progress."

                                                    U Thant

                                 *

Secretary-General? The most impossible job on Earth.

                                            Trygve Lie
                          First Secretary-General of the UN

                                 *

When Secretary-General U Thant left the UN in December 1971, he said in his farewell speech to the senior staff:
"It is not enough to work for the UN. You must also love the UN."

                                 *

Given the complexity of our planetary home and human affairs and our wrong education, it is not surprising that there should be so few people who think and deal rightly with the global destiny and • governance of this planet. Thank God, humanity has now a core of world servers and thinkers in the UN and in its specialized agencies. Please know them, listen to them, support them and pray for them.

                                 *

The title Secretary-General should be changed to:

                   Servant-General of the World.

                                 *

"To be a Permanent Representative to the UN is the hardest Ambassador's post on Earth. When the General Assembly is over,

I feel so tired and sick that I cannot eat anymore. But it is the world's most fascinating Embassy, because here you enrich yourself with the entire world and you know that you are at the center of human evolution and contributing to it."

Samir Shihabi
Ambassador of Saudi Arabia to the UN

*

"Example is not the main thing in influencing people. It is the only thing."
Albert Schweitzer

*

A foremost duty of a United Nations official is to be inspiring.

*

UN officials are the first bearers of world thoughts and feelings, the most advanced neurons of a nascent world brain, world heart and world soul.

*

The UN is the global pilgrimage of humanity. Its delegates and workers must therefore be pilgrims.

The UN is the fulfillment of a prophecy. Its members and workers must therefore be prophets.

The UN is a saintly enterprise. Its delegates and servers must therefore be saints.

*

To be a UN official is to exercise the most beautiful ministry on Earth. One is a priest, a prophet, a healer, a preacher, an artist, a writer, a scientist, an inspirer, a linguist, a believer, a universal sage and a representative and lover of this beautiful planet and of humanity. There is nothing more challenging and exalting on Earth than to work for the United Nations.

*

Those who come to the UN just for glamour or for a job are either deceived or converted.

*

The people of the UN Meditation groups in New York and in Geneva are a great new generation of world servers. They know that tomorrow will be a spiritual tomorrow.

*

Every Secretary-General, all heads of international agencies and all UN officials retiring from office should put forth their dreams, ideas, thoughts, proposals, unfinished business and visions of the future. Each should leave behind a testament and his or her proposals for a better world.

*

A golden rule for UN servants:
"The loser is one who sees a problem in every solution. The winner is he who sees a solution in every problem."

*

Why should UN workers not be poets, artists, writers and lovers of the world? Did our big reports and all our intelligence in politics, economics, science and sociology do the job? Obviously not. Why not then try the heart and the soul for a change and as a leaven?

*

The optimism of Jefferson gave the new America its spirit.

The optimism of UN servants will give the new world its spirit.

*

Oh, how I would love to see all world servants devote their whole lives, their whole energies, their whole hearts, their whole souls, beyond the call of duty, to the wonderful tasks they are entrusted with.

*

Look at the people who work for peace: how serene and happy they are.

Look at those who work for war: how insecure and guilty they look.

*

UN officials must get accustomed to perform a new, most difficult, unprecedented task: to think, to feel, to care and to act for the entire world and humanity. Some day this will become as routine as thinking, feeling, caring and acting for one's family, city, province and nation is today.

*

Oh, UN servants, do not forget that life is what you make it, that you can fill it with untold meaning and purpose. The UN gives you the most marvelous opportunities to do so. Never underestimate these opportunities. Do not be blind to them. Look out for them and they will meet you.

*

To work at the UN is to be like a seagull. You must glide up and down the stormy waves and never get wet.

*

My advice to you, Oh UN servants, is to pray, to pray very often and very intensely. Why?

First, because prayer is the image of what you wish to achieve and therefore the first step towards achieving it;

Second, because I firmly believe that this world is surrounded by unemployed spirits, saints, famous deceased sages and visionaries.

If you pray, if you open yourself to them, they will rush into you, reincarnate in you, and make you succeed. Everything you do will acquire meaning. You will be helped by them in the most mysterious, miraculous ways. Extraordinary coincidences will happen. You will become part of them and they of you. The tremendous spiritual, cosmic forces remain largely unemployed because very few people turn to them, pray to them.

*

Question to me from a Secretary:
"You really look younger than your age. How do you do it?"
I answered:
"Through prayer."
Then she asked:
"Do you really believe in prayer?"
I responded:
"Yes, most definitely. From my experience, prayer is the image of what you wish to achieve, and therefore the first step for achieving it. To achieve good things for the peace and happiness of this

beautiful world makes you feel happy and young. Nature recompenses you with youth, health and happiness."

*

To work for the UN you have to be a Machiavellian idealist: An idealist for humanity and the World, a Machiavellian to get governments to work together.

*

Anyone who goes to work for the UN needs to have the skin of an elephant, for you are expected to solve humanity's most intractable problems without any power and meaningful resources, only criticisms.

*

Sometimes, working for the UN is to have one foot in hell and the other in heaven.

*

At the UN you must have the perseverance of an ant, the skin of an elephant, the heart of a Romeo, the brain of a Socrates, the fantasy of a don Quixote and the patience of a God.

*

If I were asked what the UN needs most: Money, Authority, Power or Recognition?
My answer would be: Love, Faith, Hope, Enthusiasm, Courage, Commitment, Optimism and a Holy determination. A UN official or delegate who lacks these qualities is a displaced person at the UN.

*

Depressed, pessimistic minds cannot produce bright, positive ideas for a better world. Only exalted, optimistic minds can. This is why, at the United Nations, we cannot afford pessimists and discouraged people (literally: being without heart).
Please, UN servants, never listen to pessimists.

*

As a UN official you often do not even dare to admit any fault of the UN, for if you do it will immediately be seized by the media and the enemies of the UN. Thus, Jaime de Pines, President of the

General Assembly, mentioned in a speech to the opening of the Assembly that the UN was "in crisis". It was the headline in the media the following morning.

*

Oh world servants, I beg you, do not make your actions dependent on immediate or fast results. We have no right to expect success. We must do our maximum duty day and night, relentlessly, but the result is in the hands of God. Most of our efforts will succeed only after our death.

*

Do not look for the smallest common denominator when you work for the UN. Look for the largest.

*

The greatest danger for a world servant is to become a new type of warrior, for his Department, for a program or for a specialized agency, forgetting his or her supreme allegiance to the world and to humanity. How many times have I seen world officials fight against the creation or growth of a new world institution in order to "protect" or increase the "domain" of their own. I had to remind them that if such attitudes had prevailed at the time of the creation of their institution, they would not have a job. The world and humanity are in dire need of many more world institutions, instruments, servants, cooperation and resources. This only is worth fighting for.

*

U Thant once said to me:
"In each capital I visit I am taken to the monument of the unknown soldier, but I have never been shown a monument to the unknown peacemaker."
I commented:
"Well, the UN's tall, blue glass building is the monument to the unknown peacemakers. And someday you will see such monuments flourish all over the Earth.[14]

*

---

[14]   The Peace Monument at the University for Peace in Costa Rica has been dedicated to known and unknown peacemakers.

If a door is being closed to you by UN enemies, do not lose any time with them. Open another door. If they catch up with you at that door, open a third one. Have always a few open doors in reserve and show up where they expect you least.

*

Do not complain of other's lack of knowledge about the UN. Teach them - Go out and speak - Sit down and write

*

Since I joined the UN in 1948, I have always heard that the UN was in crisis, that its morale was low and its image at the worst. I can see only one explanation. There must be people who spread these rumors consistently in order to diminish our morale, refrain our enthusiasm and put us on the defensive. So, my dear UN colleagues, do what I do: ignore the hear-say and proceed on your own light, energy and idealism.

*

If one looks at University programs, one sees how many students are being trained in local, city, provincial, state and national adminis-tration. There are also thousands of business schools. However, nowhere are students trained for world administration. This is happening at the precise moment of history when the planet is crying for proper administration! We need a UN school of World Adminis-tration.

*

It breaks my heart when I see brilliant young men and women leave the UN for better salaries in private business. What lives and satisfactions they forego! What greater, nobler business can there be than the care of humanity and of the world?

*

A young UN television producer made the following comment to me:

"If it were not for Sir Brian Urquhart and you, I would have lost hope long ago in the UN. Thank you for the faith and inspiration you are giving us."

I answered:

"Doesn't it strike you that Sir Brian and I are among the oldest staff members of the UN? Isn't it possible that many years were necessary to make us what we are now? I remember that it was only around 1970, after 22 years of service, that I began to see clear and gain real hope. So, go on learning and the same will happen to you. It will happen to the whole world once the people have learned about the Earth, humanity and our fate in the universe."

*

When I hear a young UN official say,
"Yes, but...",
I am dismayed. Here is someone who will find excuses for not doing anything. In judging my colleagues I have a category called "the yes, but people". On the other hand, there are colleagues who are always ready to help and to do what they are asked. They are enthusiastic, they will have happy careers, they will be sought after and promoted. They do not simply have a job. They have a belief, a vocation, a calling, a mission. The others are ignored.

*

A young UN colleague complained that it was very difficult for him to get along with his superior who was all-possessive and never delegated work to him. But he liked his job very much. I said to him:
"As a UN official, you must learn to receive blows. We are real punching bags. Even if you have a good boss, during your career you will receive many blows, especially from the public."

I consider myself lucky to have survived the blows I received during my close to forty years at the UN. Perhaps at the entrance of the UN, one should inscribe these words:

You who enter here
Be prepared for any blows.
*

It is astonishing that with all the stones being thrown at the UN and the absence of encouragement, there are still people working with so much faith in it. Were they allowed to receive medals, they should receive medals of perseverance.

*

On the occasion of the fortieth anniversary of the UN, 700 staff members donated over $100,000.00 for help to the needy countries.

*

Isn't it strange that most peacemakers, prophets and visionaries never had any wealth or power and were often persecuted and killed? This phenomenon has been so consistent throughout history right into the modern times that there must be a law to it. I believe the law is this:

Evolution brings to the fore a small number of visionaries - men, women and recently also institutions such as the United Nations and the University for Peace - which have no power, no money and are being accused of idealism, naivete and irreality. These visionaries are often persecuted and killed when they become too effective. Nevertheless, they are the harbingers and pathfinders of the coming age, and sooner or later are proved to be right and do succeed.

At the same time evolution produces masses of people and institutions which cling to the past, to power, money, armies, values and education in order to assert the past and oppose the prophets and visionaries.

The reason is simple. Evolution does not want to go too fast, for it would create havoc with the great masses of people who could not take it.

Prophets, visionaries and peacemakers must therefore accept their original, difficult role as being quite natural and must not expect immediate results. But they can be very relaxed as they will win against all armies, powers, wealth and mis-education.

When I exposed this view to the depressed Secretary-General after a day of harassments, he looked at me gently and said:

"You always find a way to cheer me up."

*

Here is some of my advice to young UN world servants:

You may have no power over others, but you have power over yourself;

Keep a journal; it will help you record your journey, evaluate your progress and expand your understanding of this planet and humanity's problems;

Write down the thoughts that come to you, wherever you are, in your office, in a meeting, in a bus, in a plane, at home, during the day or the night. Remember the Latin advice: *Nullus dies, sine linea.* Not a day without a line.

Conceive constantly new ideas for a more peaceful and better world. The planet and humanity are neglected orphans, all initiatives and ideas are only for nations and for narrow groups of interests. Promote and spread these ideas, sooner or later they will fall on fertile ground;

Since you write your reports and documents in the name of the Secretary-General, try to be the Secretary-General and say and propose what he or she should say;

If you have a good idea, send it to the Secretary-General or to delegates. They or their colleagues will look into it. They need new ideas for their speeches. I know this to be true for I have worked with three Secretaries-Generals.

Be an interdisciplinary being, take interest in all UN and world affairs;

Accept eagerly to speak to the public. You learn so much when speaking. When we speak we are part of mysterious cosmic flows;

Put many irons in the fire in order to get many results; some of them require much time to warm up;

When your superiors do not listen to you, work with outside organizations, especially the non-governmental organizations accredited to the UN. They need your support, your ideas and your inspiration;

Do not do to your inferiors what you do not want your superiors to do to you;

Do not make your work and efforts depend on immediate results;

Avoid pessimists and "but people"; associate with optimists, idealists and imaginative colleagues and delegates;

Avoid and ignore narrow bureaucrats, let them have their ways; they will only drag you down to their level;

Join one of the uplifting clubs of the UN: The Pacem in Terris Society; The UN Meditation Group; The UN Writer's society; The UN Historical Society;

Remember that pessimists, complainers and nasty people have little career prospects at the UN. At best, if they are not fired, they are ignored and left aside, and their life gets ever more bitter.

Do not accuse others. Start by examining and accusing yourself.

If nobody loves you, be sure it is your own fault.

Ask yourself: What can I do for the UN? Not, what should the UN do for me.

Work for your reputation and your reputation will work for you.

I have seen young enthusiastic new staff members enter the UN. Immediately they caught sight of the higher ups. They worked hard, were always ready to help, and today I see them occupy the highest positions in the UN. Follow their examples rather than complaining.

To succeed, spare your criticisms as much as possible. To criticize others is to make enemies. I have seen some of the best young people miss their careers for their constant criticism of others, especially of those in higher positions. Follow the good example of U Thant: At best when he disliked or disapproved of someone, he remained silent.

Make a list of what you see good in your colleagues and superiors. They all have some qualities. Concentrate on those and look less at their faults. As for yourself, do the contrary.

Do not complain about adverse circumstances. Build positive ones.

Remember Gandhi's advice:

"When you have to make a decision or take a side, ask yourself if it will be to the benefit of the poorest person you ever saw."

Give the example to everyone you meet of a great UN official who believes in his or her work and in the UN, who is convinced that a peaceful and better world is possible. You will make thousands of friends for the UN and hence increase its support and effectiveness.

Prepare well your retirement in order to continue to work for peace and a better world until the last day of your life and even beyond through your works, children, disciples and writings;

Thank God every day for the tremendous privilege and luck of being a world servant. It is the most beautiful job on Earth.

*   *
*

5

The UN's Resources

In 1969, when I was Director of the UN budget, I once jotted down this note:

'The United States maintains around the world 429 major military bases, 2900 smaller bases, one million military personnel, 500,000 members of their families, 275,000 foreign workers, and spends for that between five and six billion dollars a year.

In 1969, the UN budget was 168 million dollars and the total number of international civil servants of the UN and of all its specialized agencies and world programs, including secretaries, was 40,000.'

And with that, the UN is supposed to deal with all the major problems of this planet from peace to human rights, from health to education, from development to the environment, from outer space to the atom, etc. In my view, the opponents of the UN budget should get their heads examined and be straightened out by their voters. The people should scream at their governments for their lack of serious financial support of their world organization.

*

In 1985, the UN budget was 800 million dollars shared by 160 nations. During the same year world military budgets were 800 billion dollars, i.e. a thousand times more. Of the UN budget the US was assessed 200 million dollars or one third of the cost of an atomic

Trident submarine. And yet that government complains that the UN is too costly and that the US pays too much. Historians will someday shake their heads in disbelief, especially at the gullibility of the people who swallow anything their governments want them to believe.

*

One of the best businesses on Earth:

The US pays 200 million dollars a year to the UN, gets back 600 million dollars in UN and delegation expenditures, and complains that the UN costs too much and that the US contributes too much!

Switzerland has it even better: it collects the second biggest sum from the UN and is not even a member of the UN!

*

One often hears that the UN is mismanaged.

Yes, most definitely. Here is an example: Governments pay 50 UN officials to seek world disarmament while maintaining several millions of military personnel around the world. The right word would be planetary mismanagement.

*

The UN rents each year a limousine for the President of the General Assembly during its three months session, because it is cheaper than to buy one. And each year this "outrageous" expenditure is criticized by the US media. But I have never seen a single article about the fleets of luxury cars used by the generals and officers of that country and of this planet.

*

When Ralph Bunche, a former UN Under-Secretary General and Nobel Prize winner heard attacks against the UN, he asked the attacker:

"How much do you pay for a pack a cigarettes?"

"25 cents" was the reply. (that was in the 1940's)

He then gave the person a quarter and said:

"Here is your contribution to the UN back. Now be quiet."

Today the US contribution per citizen is even less than a pack of cigarettes!

*

To demonstrate how little each of us pays for our annual contribution to the UN:
- Write down the local taxes you pay (sales taxes, property taxes);
- Write down your state taxes
- Write down your federal taxes
- Write down how much of your total taxes go to the UN and to all its specialized agencies
  (in the US it is less than 2 dollars a year).

*

To the criticism that UN officials are overpaid, my wife always asked me to have the critics call her and she would tell them how long it took her until she could afford a dishwashing machine.

As a matter of fact, the salaries are so unattractive for certain countries that they pay extra subsidies to their nationals to make it worthwhile to expatriate themselves and work in the high-cost cities of the UN and of its specialized agencies. The US pays their nationals salary differentials when they return home

*

During the early history of the US, some of the American states did not pay their dues to the government in Washington when they did not like it or wanted to exercise pressure. The same is happening to the UN today. This remark by George Washington applies fully today to the world:

"The primary cause of all disorders lies in the different state governments and in the tenacity of that power which pervades the whole of their systems."

*

5 December, 1985

The UN received today its thirty millionth visitor, a student from Gardner High School in New Jersey.

The UN receives an average of 1500 visitors a day and gives tours in twenty four languages, including sign language.

Sadly enough, Sunday tours have been abolished due to financial restrictions imposed upon the UN by the non-payment of the US contribution.

*

It is incredible what the UN has done to inform the people about the conditions of the world and of humanity. This alone would merit ten times the insignificant sums spent on it.

*

"If one compares the objectives of the United Nations with its means, it would not be exaggerated to say that the UN institutions are expected to ensure humanity's happiness for a few hundred million dollars"

Maurice Bertrand
external UN Inspector

*

It would be good to publish statistics on what national health departments spend and what the World Health Organization spends, and to do the same for all UN agencies and world programs. The results would be staggering. They would reveal how little is being done for the planet and for humanity, and how much for its subdivisions and subordinate entities. Politicians should have sleepless nights. No wonder that the world is in such a mess. We are the most distorted and misguided budgeted planet in the universe.

*

When the City of Philadelphia decided to celebrate the bicentennial of the US constitution, its council immediately approved a budget of 100 million dollars for the celebration. When the Secretary-General of the United Nations proposed that the world celebrate the fortieth anniversary of the UN, the US and the USSR agreed only on the condition that it would not cost anything.

The world and humanity are always the orphans. Don't the people have the right to their world celebrations? Will it be the same for the celebration of the fiftieth anniversary of the UN and of the Bimillennium?

*

The UN is the lowest paid and least well equipped police officer on Earth.

*

UNESCO reports that nations spend more money on teaching international relations in universities than they spend on the entire

United Nations and its thirty-two specialized agencies! There is something basically wrong with that.

*

If only the huge military budgets of this planet could be subjected to the same extreme scrutiny as is the tiny budget of the United Nations. Astronomic sums would be spared to the taxpayers and much waste to this planet.

*

One of the preferred stances of UN-haters is lack of coordination among UN agencies. My God, why don't they direct their attention to the lack of coordination between governments and within governments? There they would find billions of dollars of potential savings rather than the few hundred thousand dollars they could squeeze out of the ridiculous budgets of the world agencies. One thinks one is dreaming when one hears the nonsense of these people. But of course, they are not interested in facts. They are only interested in hating and in destroying and keeping secure their benefits from the present world chaos.

*

To those who accuse the UN of being a talk-shop one should answer:

"There is more glory in killing war with words than in killing."
St. Augustine

*

In 1970, during the twenty-fifth anniversary of the UN, the Republican administration of the US wanted to reduce its contribution to the UN budget from 33 percent to 25 percent. Secretary-General U Thant proposed to Ambassador George Bush that the US contribution be reduced to 15%, but the US refused, arguing that it would lose too much influence in the UN.

An added reason was probably also that with such a low percentage the US would lose the opportunity to complain and to exercise pressure on political issues by refusing to pay. The latter is a beloved technique of the big powers, an additional veto.

*

"The only mistake we made in San Francisco when adopting the Charter of the UN was not to include a veto on the budget."

Ambassador Malik
USSR

*

In 1972, during a visit of the Secretary-General to China, Premier Zhou En Lai asked him how much the US contributed to the UN? (25%); The USSR? (14%); and China? (6%).

Zhou En Lai retorted:

"This must be changed. The Chinese contribution must be substantially increased, because as the Americans say:

'He who pays the fiddler, calls the tune' "
*

Zhou En Lai also asked the Secretary-General:

"Why do all world agencies have their seats in New York, Washington, Paris, London, Geneva, Rome, The Hague, etc? Why is not a single one located in the poor countries, for example here in Asia, where two-thirds of the world's population live? Don't we count in the world? Couldn't the Security Council meet once in awhile in our area? We would be happy to receive it in China, or in any other country of Asia."

That was in 1972. Twenty years later, the situation is still the same. After that conversation I convinced the Secretary-General to convene the Security Council in other capitals, closer to the people and trouble spots. Indeed, it met shortly thereafter in Addis Ababa and in Panama. But when I left the Secretary-General's office, this policy stopped and was never resumed. Zhou En Lai, for his part, obtained that the newly created UN Environment Program be established in Nairobi, Kenya. Since then also, China uses its veto in the Security Council to ensure that new Secretary-Generals be appointed mostly from other than western countries.

*

The US contribution to the UN budget could be easily met by moving the UN's seat to a country like Costa Rica where costs would be only 1/3 or 1/4. Costa Rica moreover would merit it, since it is the first country on Earth which has outlawed the military.

*

98

The UN budget, considered excessive by the western countries, could be easily reduced if there were not the high costs of cities like New York, Geneva and Paris. Someone should calculate the savings which could be made by transferring some world agencies to low-cost countries.

*

Among the US attacks against UNESCO there is the accusation of bad administration and financial mismanagement. But the head of UNESCO's administration and financial services was an American, a former colleague of mine at the UN budget. When I met him, I asked: "Why don't you go and testify before the US Congress"? He shrugged his shoulders and answered: "Well, you know what politics are".

As a matter of fact most of the administrative and financial services of the UN agencies are headed by Americans.

*

The UN and its specialized agencies (except the International Bank) are the only governmental bodies on this planet which cannot borrow money. On the contrary member-governments often owe them money.

*

When the Secretary-General told me that he would answer questions on the budget during a press conference after the General Assembly, I advised him:

"If a journalist asks you a question about the UN budget, you could put on a surprised face and ask them : what budget? You don't call the trickle of resources given to the UN a budget, I hope."

*

The entire documentation published by the UN in one year in four languages for 160[15] member states with no advertising, on practically every world problem under the sun amounts to less paper than **one** Sunday edition of the *New York Times*! But guess who is

---

[15]   In 1992: 179

criticized in the media, including the *New York Times*, for being a paper-mill?

*

The *New York Times* once published the photo of a small wagon filled with paper being pushed into the UN, accusing the organization of being a paper-mill. I wrote them a letter asking them to publish the information in the preceding paragraph. They never did.

It reminds me of Margaret Mead's remark that someone should publish a newspaper with the letters from readers rejected by the *New York Times*.

Freedom of information?! Yes, freedom for those who own the media.

*

One often hears criticism in western democracies that the UN is dominated by its numerous poor member countries. This is no criticism, it is sheer cynicism. The UN system is in reality dominated by the western countries:

1.   Through the veto powers in the Security Council;

2.   Through their special voting powers in the International Bank and Monetary Fund;

3.   Through their insistence that UN decisions should be taken by consensus (when it suits them);

4.   Through the location of the UN, its main offices and all of the specialized agencies in western countries where they can be easily controlled;

5.   Through the refusal or delay in paying their contributions, and threats to cut bilateral aid, to exercise pressure on voting;

6.   Their refusal to create any new UN institutions or programs even when they are sorely needed;[16]

There may be other examples unknown to someone as naïve as me.

*

---

[16]   See chapter 10, The UN and the Future.

Another advantage for the rich countries of keeping the seats of world agencies in western, high-cost capitals, is that it renders almost impossible for the indigenous people of the world to be represented as non-governmental organizations and to express their voice and perceptions in the world fora.

*

Jean Monnet, when laying down the outlines of the European Community of which. he was the father, rejected the principle of voluntary contributions by member states, the system retained for the UN. He held that it would not work and obtained a European obligatory tax on value added in production and imports.[17] This is why the European Community was never threatened by the withholding of contributions, and disposes over adequate resources. A similar reform must be introduced whereby the UN will be financed with a world tax on arms production or sales, or tax on alcohol or cigarettes, or an additional levy on postage stamps by all countries. The time is long overdue for such an indispensable reform.

*

Everybody speaks of the cost of the UN, but seldom does one hear any mention of the savings and benefits accruing from it to the nations and to the world:

For example the eradication of smallpox from the surface of the Earth saved governments two billion dollars a year, more than the total cost of the UN and of all its specialized agencies and world programs. This figure represents only direct savings: border controls, immunization treatment, etc. But think also of the indirect benefits:

In India, for example, the eradication of smallpox reduced the number of new blind people by fifty percent.

---

[17] Sixty percent of the resources of the EEC come from a surcharge on the value added tax, 22 percent from customs duties and 9 percent from contributions of member countries based on the Gross National Product. In 1990 the EEC had a budget of 74.4 billion dollars.

Think also of the expenses spared the world by solving more than one hundred conflicts since 1945.

Think of the savings to governments which could discontinue their international statistical publications and world studies and surveys, since the United Nations is providing them to all. The statistical and data collection work of the UN system would merit a Nobel Prize. When I joined the UN in 1948, we did not even know how many people lived on this planet. Today, the statistical yearbooks and publications of the UN system cover an enormous table. All the world statistics used in schools, universities, in the media and in governments are the product of the United Nation's statistical services.

Think of the savings to many small countries who are able to handle their diplomacy right at the UN and do not have to establish costly diplomatic services in all countries.

Think of the disasters spared the world by warning it of the population explosion, the deterioration of the environment, desertification, deforestation, and many other global menaces, the latest being climatic changes and the aging of the population.

As an example:

In 1970, during the twenty-fifth anniversary of the UN, the estimate of the world population in the year 2000 was 7.3 billion people. In 1985, during the fortieth anniversary, the estimate was down to 6.1 billion, thanks largely to the UN's global warnings, world population conferences and direct assistance to poor countries by the UN Fund for Population Activities.

It is fashionable to criticize the UN and never say a good word about it. In reality, it is one of the cheapest and most effective organizations on Earth, given its meager resources and lack of power.

*

During a speech I gave to visitors at the UN, I noticed that the Dag Hammarskjöld auditorium was freezing. I pitied the elderly persons in the audience and inquired why the room was not heated. I was told that it was for budgetary restrictions since the US had not paid its dues. I thought sadly:

"Is there one room in the Pentagon or in any military establishment on Earth that would ever be left unheated because of budgetary restrictions?"

And I asked God:

"Why is it that peace is always so blatantly short-measured on this planet? Are we fools to believe in peace and to work for it? Why do you allow this to happen to your servants on your beautiful planet?"

*

Secretary-General Perez de Cuellar complained to me:

"It is so cold in my office."

I told him:

"They are cutting down heat in order to save money, since the US does not pay its contribution. The Dag Hammarskjöld auditorium is also without heat. I wonder if there is one military establishment on this planet that has ever been forced to reduce its heat. This is the sad world in which we live."

*

There are 556 soldiers per 100,000 people on this planet
There are 85 doctors per 100,000 people
There is 1 world servant per 100,000 people

*

The world spends 1800 times more on military personnel than on UN peace-keeping forces.

*

The onslaught of some US members of Congress against the minuscule United Nations budget reminds me of a remark by Mr. Tishman, the skyscraper builder, a staunch supporter of the UN, when in 1970 a similar anti-UN mood was raging in Congress. He said to me: "Under US federal law, the cities of this country are required to have balanced budgets and cannot have any budgetary deficits. The same applies to the United Nations which does not even have the right to borrow money. And the same governments who lay down these rules indulge in the most astronomic deficits and borrowing operations! You should remind them of their misbehavior when they have the nerve to criticize the UN. The UN should be given borrowing capacity and nations should be required to balance their budgets."

*

In 1970, when Mr. Waldheim became Secretary-General, one of his first objectives was to get the United Nations debt settled. I told him that it was not a problem to worry about. It was mainly owed to countries which had participated in peace-keeping operations in the Congo, mostly Nordic countries, without the approval of some members of the Security council who refused to pay. The countries to whom the money was due did not press for payment and would not declare the UN in bankruptcy. Nevertheless it remained a main issue on his mind. When he spoke for the first time before the US Congress, he mentioned the problem and his eagerness to see it solved. At the evening cocktail, Senator Fullbright asked him how much this debt was. Mr. Waldheim gave him the figure: 3 million dollars. Fullbright looked at him with utter surprise and said:

"Mr. Secretary-General, if the debt of the United States amounted to that sum, I would pledge myself to crawl on my knees from the Washington monument to Capitol Hill, burning a candle at each step to thank God!"

*

Ever since I joined the United Nations I have known the Organization to be in "crisis". I sometimes feel that this "crisis status" is systematically cultivated in order to prevent the Organization from becoming too popular with the public and from acquiring real strength.

*

History should never forget that in the Year of Grace 1986, the International Year of Peace, the Congress of a major country which spends hundreds of billions of dollars a year on deadly weapons, 29 billion dollars on tobacco and 475 million dollars on pornography, decided not to pay its 200 million dollars contribution to the United Nations.

*

There is little talk in the US media of the financial crisis provoked by the US. Why? Because at a time when everything is couched in billions, the challenge of a yearly contribution of 200 million dollars to a world-wide organization would be considered ridiculous even by an uninformed public. You cannot fool the public to that extent.

*

Question of a Pentagon General to his secretary:
"What comes after trillion?"

*

The only advantage I see in the small budgets of the UN and of the specialized agencies is that if a major contributor wants to leave them, they will be perfectly able to survive. The precedents of the departure of the US from the ILO and UNESCO are good examples. Other governments are ready to chip in, but it is a sad comment on the state of affairs on this planet.

*

I found this note of 7 May 1969, when I became Director of the UN budget.
"The US press reports that the Pentagon has "forgotten" or has made a mistake of one and a half billion dollars in its anti-ballistic defense budget!"
If the UN had "forgotten" or made a budgetary mistake of a million dollars, it would come under severe criticism.

*

Officials who deal with the UN budget in Washington call it "petty cash". That is exactly what it is. And with this grotesque petty cash, the UN is expected to solve all the world's problems from war to terrorism, from drug abuse to the environment, from human rights to racial equality and what have you not.

*

The US Congress should hold hearings on how the Executive branch uses its non-payments of dues to the UN and to its agencies, or pays only at particular moments, and cuts foreign aid to exercise pressure on other governments to change their UN votes. The votes on China's representation and on the Iraq-Kuwait crisis would be particularly revealing.

Oh, but I forgot, there is the famous "reason of state"! George Washington would revolt against such a situation, but sadly there are no longer any George Washingtons

*

Passage from a convocation to a world conference of religions for peace in London:

"Almost all the world religions define themselves as universal, i.e. as spiritual communities reaching right across all nations, races, and continents. This implies that their ministers - ideally - ought to be above all partiality and group-interests. No politician, except perhaps a handful of those working in global institutions such as the UN, can afford to show this type of disinterest since he or she is obliged to represent the needs and demands of those to whom he is answerable. He must serve his community, department, or office. Even if he serves the entire country or nation, his job is to defend his country's interest, if necessary against that of other countries or nations. If he does not do so, he is not considered a good politician."

In this text lies the reason of the reluctance of governments to let the United Nations and its agencies grow to the vigor required by current global evolution: Those who can afford to reach right across all nations, races and continents are supposed to remain a handful only. It is therefore up to the people to request urgent changes.

*

Letter of a major Paris publisher to Claudine Brelet, a former official of the World Health Organization, who had submitted to them the manuscript of a book entitled *"Planet of the United Nations"*:

"There is no market for such a book in France. But if you would write a book about the malfunctioning of the UN and its waste of money, we would consider it."[18]

I got similar remarks when I circulated my first manuscript on happiness. I even got this answer:

"We will never publish a book favorable to the UN"

*

---

[18]   1992: the book still remains unpublished.

When I was Director of the UN Budget, I made the following proposals to introduce a greater justice in the sharing of UN costs, now based entirely on the gross national product of member countries:

1.   A separate budget should be established for languages. There is no reason why countries whose language is not one of the working languages of the UN should share in their costs;

2.   The countries where the seats of the UN and of its agencies are located should pay more, since they derive substantial revenues from the expenses of the UN and of the delegations established at those seats;

3.   Cost comparisons should be made to help delegates assess the effects of huge costs of living in certain cities of the western countries where UN agencies are located;

4.   Contributions to the UN budget by member governments should no longer be included in the budgets of "Foreign Affairs". Their part in these budgets is sometimes high and as a result the Ministries of Foreign Affairs are not eager to defend them before their Parliaments.   Contributions to world agencies should become a separate chapter in national budgets;

5.   There should be a capital budget for the UN to permit the amortization of heavy capital expenditures, such as modern computers for world data, satellite systems and other rapid telecommunications, modernization of buildings, etc.

6.   Every year the General Assembly should receive a document comparing the increases in the budgets of nations, especially military budgets, and the budgets of the world agencies.

A quarter of a century later, to my knowledge, none of these proposals has been adopted.

*

The so-called financial "crisis" of the UN is nothing new. I knew it in its full swing in 1969-70 as the newly appointed Director of the budget. At that time, the four big powers, led by the United States, deposited memoranda with Secretary-General U Thant, requesting a three year freeze on the growth of the UN budget, as they still do today.

I recommended to the Secretary-General the following steps:

1. Ask them what they criticize and object to specifically.

2. If it is the level of expenses, then why don't you compare the tiny, insignificant budget of the UN with the national budgets of the US, the USSR, France and the UK? You will see what ridiculous sums are devoted to peace and to needed growing world cooperation.

3. Why don't you compare the UN budget in particular with your military expenditures and their growth? Why not freeze the latter? You would save infinitely more.

4. What do your contributions to the UN budget represent per American, per Russian, per Frenchman, per Englishman? What was that contribution in 1946?

5. What was the increase in taxes per capita in your countries since the end of World War II? Compare this with the percentage growth of the UN budget.

6. What are the UN expenditures per capita for the entire world?

7. Give them a number of typical comparisons: the UN budget is no bigger than the budget of the Fire Department of New York City, than the budget of the military bands and heating bill of the US Army, than the cost of a nuclear submarine, than one day of the Vietnam war.

8. Tell them to make a study of the savings accrued to them, thanks to the UN.

9.   Why must the UN balance its budget and live from hand to mouth when nations borrow colossal sums of money and incur astronomical debts?

10.   Why do you burden your people with innumerable taxes and do not allow the tiniest world levy to help defray common world services and save the environment?

11.   Why don't you reduce your incessant, numerous and excessive controls over the UN budget which has become the most controlled budget on Earth?

12.   What specific suggestions do you have?"

I added:
"If I were you, I would throw these memoranda in the waste basket. The big powers do not have the right to address to you such requests."

Soon thereafter the budget freeze idea was abandoned and I was "transferred" to the position of Director of the Executive Office of the Secretary-General. When I started my job with U Thant, he said to me:
"You will be happier here than in the budget."

How right he was. We did many wonderful things together, and each year when he received the usual protest notes from the big powers against UN budget increases, he threw them in the waste basket. As for me, I hold the record for having been the shortest lived budget director of the UN.

*

Global problems are so pressing and so mounting, and global cooperation and agencies are so pathetically underfinanced that it has become imperative in the interest of human survival and of our planet to hold a world conference on the financing of global cooperation.

*

The US is unable to finance the construction of an atomic particle splitter the size of the European CERN, financed by all European countries. Just imagine what the world could do if it decided to finance jointly some great common projects instead of wasting colossal sums in endless national duplications. Nations have done it only once: for the eradication of smallpox. This was a resounding success. One UN world peace-keeping force, with contributions by all nations on Earth, would save this planet the colossal sum of a thousand billion dollars!

*

I wish the UN would publish an annual report on the world's present budget, showing what 179 national governments spend on all major categories of public expense. It would be a most revealing, shocking document. It would be glaring proof of the mismanagement of this planet, and of the madness of the present system of sovereign nation-states.

*

There were great difficulties during the last part of the twentieth century to shift the minds and interests of the people from deeply entrenched national concerns to world thinking and concerns. I hope my testament, and especially this chapter, will illustrate the situation for future generations and historians.

*　　*
*

6

The UN and I

"Take up one idea. Make that one idea your life. Think of it, dream of it. Live on the idea. Let the brain, the muscles, nerves, every part of your body be full of that idea, and just leave every other idea alone. This is the way great spiritual giants are produced."

Vivekananda

My own "one idea" was that life is divine, a true miracle. The fulfillment of life requires peace. The UN is the universal instrument of peace. Therefore, I let my brain, muscles, nerves, heart and soul become full of the UN.

*

Every day I ask God: What more can I do for the peace and happiness of this world? And the answer invariably is: Go to the UN and work, work, work.

*

I pray and thank God every day for the United Nations.

*

What I would have missed in my life if I hadn't worked for the UN! I should rewrite in golden letters the essay on world government which opened to me the doors of the UN as a young man.

*

My God, how dearly I have loved this planet and humanity! Please allow me to come back as a spirit to provoke the heads of states into the right directions!

*

It is not easy to be a human, surrounded by all the mysteries of the universe, of life and of death. It is good, therefore, to help each other, to cooperate, to stick together as a human race. Each one of us can do so much: encourage and inspire others, see a quality in all, radiate happiness and zest for life. What a result, what a validation and elevation of humanity it would be, multiplied by 5 billion people! This is what I have tried to prove at the UN.

*

Having felt it myself since childhood, I have always tried to convey to my human brothers and sisters the consciousness that life is a miracle, a divine phenomenon and that each of us is a unique miracle never to be repeated again in all eternity. The UN has reinforced this fundamental belief in me.

*

To be a minstrel of peace, a knight of the United Nations and of world brotherhood, that was my wonderful fate. I invite all my human brothers and sisters on Earth to join me in this universal knighthood.

*

If only through my writings, actions, example and speeches I could make warring and armed nations feel ashamed of themselves!

*

I have often been asked:
"How do you keep so young?"
I always reply:
"Because I work for humanity and for the world. It is such a huge, long, unfinished job that God keeps me young in order not to lose one of His workers."

*

As a child I hated to see problems which were a blemish to the peace, beauty and happiness of the world.

God heard me and made me work for the UN where one sees all the blemishes of the world.

So I decided to challenge these world blemishes and I became a happy man, because to remove these blemishes is to contribute to the peace, beauty and happiness of the world. I fulfilled the cosmic role ingrained in me.

*

I love this passage from a letter of William Penn:

"There is one great God and Power that has made the world and all things therein, to whom you and I and all people owe their being and well being, and to whom you and I must one day give an account for all that we do in this world: this great God has written his law in our hearts, by which we are taught and commanded to love and help do good to one another and not to do harm and mischief unto one another.

Now this great God has been pleased to make me concerned in your parts of the world..."

I would end it for my part as follows:

"Now this great God has been pleased to make me concerned with the world and to place me in the United Nations..."

*

From a reader:

"I do hope that my letter reaches you, although I am uncertain whether you are still at the UN. I feel that if your health is good, that is where you will be found."

Right she was!

*

A German delegate reminded me of a remark I made to her twenty years ago:

"I am not interested so much whether there will or will not be a world Cocoa agreement under UN auspices. I am interested in observing and seeing the human destiny unfold on the world scene of the UN."

*

I would like my love for the UN to resound from one end of the Earth to the other.

*

My faith in the UN derives from my unfailing belief that the universe and God are on our side and mysteriously guide and support us even through our traumas and mistakes. World cooperation is therefore the key to our cosmic success, and non-cooperation is its main obstacle.

*

My capacity for life, my enthusiasm for life, my devotion to a better world, my many years of service at the UN, the places where I labored, the people I met, the inspirations I received, my innumerable ideas, all this was the will of God. As a tiny manifestation of life in the vast universe, I had no merit. I was merely a willing, happy instrument of the universe, of humanity, of the Earth and of God. This is what I was born for. This is what all humans are born for.

*

As long as the sun will shine on me and on my grave, I will defend and love the United Nations.

*

For me the UN is a star of hope hovering above the Earth. It is there to stay and will never fade. God and the Saints will help it shine until at long last peace will reign on Earth.

*

What was my task at the UN?
To work as a gardener in the garden of God. It was heavenly work. I tried hard. Some of my flowers grew beautifully. Others did not and withered away. It was all in the hands of God.

*

I feel as happy in the UN as Thoreau was at Walden Pond, and Burroughs in his slab house in Esopus. For me, the UN is the house of God, the greatest house of hope on this planet.

*

My mother, the milliner, had many materials which she endlessly rearranged into different, beautiful hats for the joy of her customers.

I have at my disposal many materials given to me by the UN. I rearrange them endlessly into different, beautiful achievements for the benefit of humanity and of the Earth.

*

As a child, I often looked out of my window at the stars and the moon, and I prayed to God:

Oh God, let me be on top of the world.

He fulfilled my dream. During all my adult life I was at the UN, on top of the world.

Ask yourself, what was your dream as a child, your dearest, deepest dream, the one you had when you looked at the stars and the moon and spoke to God?

*

"The world is my country. Humanity is my family. To do good is my religion."

Thomas Paine

"The Earth is but one country, and humans are its citizens."
Baha'u'llah

"The entire Earth is my home and the universe is my country."
Darshan Singh

*

I have the most beautiful profession on Earth: that of a world servant, a servant of all the people and of the planet.

*

I will never commit the grievous sin of losing faith in humanity.

*

I was once asked:

"What astonished you most in the UN?"

I answered:

"That I, the son of a poor hatmaker from Alsace-Lorraine, was allowed to work there for 38 years and to become an Assistant-Secretary-General."

*

After more than three decades of work for the first universal organization, my love for it is such that I pray all my human brothers and sisters to help it, to understand it and to love it. You will not be disappointed. You will be helping a better world and will feel happy in return.

*

I will never stop trying to do, each day, more for this beautiful planet and for humanity than the day before.

*

I want to use all my brain, all my heart, all my soul and all my strength to beg the people to love this planet, to love humanity, to love God and the UN.

*

If one really loves someone or something, one must at least be ready to forgive, if not love their shortcomings. I have applied this rule to my love for humanity and for the UN. Why should I insist on a perfect planet, a perfect humanity, a perfect UN, a perfect wife and perfect children, when I myself am not perfect?

*

I am enthusiastic about life
I am enthusiastic about peace
I am enthusiastic about the UN
I am enthusiastic about this planet.

*

I would be ready to work in hell for peace and for the United Nations, but would prefer to do it in heaven!

*

After a speech in which I mentioned that I came from a hat-maker's family and that I was a fully trained hatmaker, a listener commented:

"You never ceased to be a hatmaker. At the UN you are trying to make a hat fitting the whole world."

*

A nice message I received on Valentine's Day:

"Thank you for all you have done and are doing to bring the consciousness of God's peace and love to this world."

*

I am a product, a child of the United Nations. Anyone who wishes to become a loving universal being as I have become should get to know our mother, the United Nations.

*

A UN colleague said to me:

"If there were only five people like you at the UN, what a change this would make!"

I looked at him sternly and commented:

"Why did you add four excuses to not being one of the five yourself?"

I have lived and worked in the United Nations for almost forty years. I wonder sometimes, if I have given it all my care, all my love, all my mind and all my soul.

When I leave the UN, I will ask it for forgiveness.

*

After I had won a long and difficult battle for the creation of a UN institution to help the poor countries, a British delegate had this dismal comment:

"You won, but we made you lose three years of your life."

*

Sometimes after several years, when I meet a western delegate who fought obstinately against the creation or strengthening of UN mechanisms for a better world, I ask this question:

"Don't you think we should suppress, say the regional banks created at the behest of the UN?"

The common reaction is:

"You must be crazy. They are eminently useful."

Whereupon I smile and say:

"Well, do you remember how bitterly you fought their creation years ago?"

*

Once I was asked by my boss to defend one of my ideas in a private meeting of western delegates who opposed the idea stubbornly. I made an impassioned speech, at the end of which the German delegate, to the consternation of his western colleagues, agreed with me and gave his approval.

That evening, at a diplomatic reception, this same delegate, who had lost an arm as a Panzer commander in World War II, said to me:

"I broke the instructions of my government, but I wanted to give my vote to an honest man who had the courage to defend his opinion and who knew how to move and convince me with his passionate speech for a better world."

*

One of my sons, François, who works for the UN Development Program, asked me:

"Dad, why do you have all these crazy ideas? Can't you ever stop?"

I answered:

"If I had not had the crazy idea of creating major development instruments for the poor countries at the UN, you and several thousand of your colleagues would not have a job at the UN today."

He believed me, when at the fortieth anniversary of the UNDP, I was invited to speak to the staff as one of the last living pioneers of the program. I donated and inaugurated on that occasion a bust of Paul Hoffman, the first Administrator of the UNDP, saying:

"Every time you pass by this bust, I want you to remember his words and example: 'Have an ideal, have a dream and work for it relentlessly.'"

*

Whenever I complete a task successfully or fulfill a dream or idea at the UN, I move to another seemingly impossible challenge. That is why today I am nurturing the fledgling infancy of the University for Peace.

*

To have worked for the UN was an incredible privilege and benediction.

God placed me in my particular position at the UN to work for humanity, and all cosmic forces assisted me. I can feel it most definitely.

Oh God, do not let some misguided people destroy the work of all my life and of so many of my colleagues.

*

I am in passion with life, with humanity and with this beautiful planet. I am and will always remain a passionate advocate of the UN. I will never refuse my action, thought, heart and soul to the first universal organization on this planet.

*

If there should remain only one person on Earth who believes in the UN, it will be me.

*

Each time I see and chat with Secretary-General Perez de Cuellar, I like myself better, because he makes me feel great.

*

When I was a young UN official I thought that the following sign should be placed at the entrance of the UN:

"You who enter here, leave all hope."

Today I would say:

"You who enter here, never leave hope."

*

A reviewer of my book *"What War Taught Me About Peace"*, apologized for criticizing me:

"You have certainly earned your place among the immortals of the UN, but I had to underline that you are always all-supportive of the UN and never find fault with it. I believe you should help in underlining and redressing what is wrong with the UN."

I answered:

"You are indeed right. But there are so many people who criticize the UN that I feel it my duty to counter their negative influence by stressing the good aspects of the UN which they ignore. Also, if I were to voice the slightest criticism, the UN haters would jump on it and proclaim: 'You see, even such a defender of the UN as Robert Muller is critical.' They would use it to undermine the UN".

I have taken a similar stand in this testament. The UN enemies will seek in vain arguments and ammunition for their evil designs. Once **they** have become objective, I will also be ready to discuss honestly the shortcomings of the UN.

*

We must make the UN the determining agent of change for a peaceful and better world. We cannot allow anything to happen to it. We owe it to the 30 million dead of World War II.

Since I was miraculously saved during that war, my life became a challenge to all wars. I will win, for myself, for my dead comrades, for my children and grandchildren, for our beautiful planet and for its extraordinary human race.

*

The UN is the will and product of evolution, so much so that its worst enemies cannot touch it. Nor can they touch or discourage me.

*

People often tell me: "You have done so much for the United Nations." In reality, they will never know how little I did and how much the UN has done for me. It was a beautiful love story of a mother for her child. I hope to write as much as I can about it in order to inspire others.

*

My love for the UN will not die with me. It will continue to live through my writings, through the young UN officials they will inspire, through the students I am now teaching at the University for Peace.

*

In my work at the UN, in my life in general, I had a whole range of intentions, a vast canvass of ideas, visions and actions. I was a world smith, with hundreds of irons in the fire, a hatmaker with every conceivable material, a chef disposing over innumerable culinary ingredients, a painter with all the gamut of colors, a composer with an infinity of notes.

We are all smiths, hatmakers, chefs, painters and composers of life, of peace and of a better world.

*

Sometimes people accuse me for being overenthusiastic about the UN. My answer is:

"In reality, I do not care excessively about the UN. It is only an institution which is as good as the life, heart and spirit of the people who work for it. What I really care for is human happiness, and fulfillment. Since the UN is fighting for peace world-wide, and since peace is the precondition to happiness, I am ready to fight for the UN until my death, and possibly even after it."

*

Out of devotion arises an habitual faith which makes the object of devotion part of your life.

Select therefore a worthy object of devotion: God, your family, your home, your profession, peace, justice, art, a better world.

I have made this planet, humanity and the United Nations the objects of my devotion and they became part of my life.

*

When I was a little boy I considered life to be divine and I had a sense of wonder at the whole Creation around me.

Then I was taught to hate other nations, I knew war and the horrors done by men to God's Creation.

Then God led me to the United Nations and I learned to love the entire Earth and all humanity.

I ended where I had started: I considered life to be divine and I regained my sense of wonder at the whole Creation.

*

Love is the radiance of happiness. I have loved the United Nations, the Earth and humanity, and my secretary called me "sunshine man".

*

Among the many epithets given to me during my years at the UN, the following were my preferred ones:

Purushottama, given to me by *Sri Chinmoy*: "The one who seeks the origin and reason of all things".

Koogun Deyo - Spider Boy, given to me by the Hopi Indians: "The one who is to catch all evil in his web and throw it far into the universe".

*

I met a former UN colleague whom I had not seen for years. He had left the UN to become a Professor of political science which paid him a better salary. I asked him how he was doing. He answered: "Fine, but I am often mad at you because you cross my way."

I expressed surprise:

"But we have not seen each other for years!"

"Yes, he replied, but often my students brandish your books, your speeches and your ideas which challenge the current teachings of political science."

His remark made my day!

*

From a letter by one of my readers:

"I have only read 127 pages of your book *New Genesis, Shaping a Global Spirituality,* but feel compelled to write now. You are such a warm relief. We have been looking with such anxiety and despair to our Washington government, while our saviour, the United Nations, sits quietly aside, protecting us with love. Your revelation is truly one of hope that restores my faith in our great country."

*

Many people try to make a hero out of me! Don't they know that I want every human person to be a hero? To single me out as an exception is to defeat my efforts, making it difficult for ordinary people to be like me.

*

I dream all that can be dreamt
I believe all that can be believed
I hope all that can be hoped
I do all that can be done
I endure all that can be endured

Those were my guiding rules in the United Nations.

*

I am not only a United Nations official, I am principally an enthusiast, an advocate, a defender of life.

I am not only an international civil servant, I am a server of God, of life, of the universe, of this planet and of humanity.

*

I regret that I have only one life to devote to the UN, to the world and to humanity. But perhaps through my writings I will remain alive a little longer, defending the UN and seeking for it the love and understanding of all.

*

My wife often asks me: "Why do you spend so much time autographing books?"

My reply is:

"Because an autographed book has a better chance to survive. Perhaps, after my death some of my books might show up in garage sales and be read by young people who will be inspired to pursue my work and implement my ideas."

*

I do not think so much about what I do for the UN and humanity, but rather what the UN and humanity do for me. What I do is indeed very little compared with what they do for me. In order to compensate for the difference, I ask myself constantly the question:

What more can I do for the UN and for humanity?

*

Even if the whole world were against the UN, I would defend it with all my strength, all my soul and all my heart because it was born from the 30 million dead of World War II and it is our best chance for a better world.

*

One of the nicest epithets I ever received came from one of my uncles, a retired railroad man who once said to me:

"You are a Weltverbesserer!"

(You are a world improver!)

*

One of the contributions of my life was to help incorporate all aspects of life and of our planetary home into the UN, and the UN into our lives and homes.

*

I am one of the rare human beings who after two contradictory national programmings was lucky to be rightly reprogrammed by the United Nations as a member of the human family and as an inhabitant of planet Earth.

*

The United Nations was for me a universal home, the most extraordinary school on Earth. It aggrandized me from a narrow national being (once French, once German) to belonging to the entire planet and human family. This is why I pray so much that the United Nations will be transformed into the united nation of all peoples of this Earth.

*

I have seen evolution at work through the United Nations. I have seen emerge in it new challenges and crises, unprecedented preoccupations and opportunities in human history. Within its workings, I have seen how humanity is progressively finding its way on this planet, toddling along amidst many difficulties, idiosyncrasies and obstacles, but always on an upward path. It is a very fascinating story.

*

All the great virtues - peace, spirituality, knowledge, justice, wisdom - are best illustrated by the example of great lives. This is why the University for Peace has launched a series of symposia held at the United Nations, entitled:
"Great Visionaries of Peace".
As Albert Schweitzer said:
"Example is not the main thing in influencing people. It is the only thing."
Like my Alsatian compatriot I tried to make my life an example too.

*

Whether I like it or not, I will be considered as a kind of UN Socrates, Confucius or Buddha of modern times, but I do not deserve this merit whatsoever. I was simply an observer, a child, a product, a fruit of the searches and unceasing questions and trials of the human race in the UN and in its various agencies.

*

124

I dream to be an elder of the UN, living on a hill and telling the beautiful story of my life and vision of a better world before I return to Mother Earth.[19]

*

My only true friends in life were those who shared the same passion and concern for the world, for humanity and for the United Nations. I was never able to cultivate any other real friendships.

*

A comment of the President of the Association of the Grand Orient of France in New York, after hearing me speak to his society:
"In sixty minutes I learned more about the UN than from reading the *New York Times* for forty years."

*

Since I underestimated the number of heads of states who would attend the fortieth anniversary commemoration of the UN by fifteen percent, I decided to increase my optimism by the same percentage. Otherwise, I felt I would fall behind reality and lose my unofficial title of:

"Optimist in residence at the UN".

*

Even if I remained alone in the world to believe in the UN, I would not budge an inch from my belief, for my conscience and God tell me that I am right. Christ was also right and alone; even Peter failed Him. And yet Christ is still alive amongst us. So too will the United Nations, or its successor, until the Gospels are fulfilled.

*

---

[19]   This dream was fulfilled: In March of 1991, on my 68th birthday, I acquired a hill adjacent to the University for Peace in Costa Rica with a tiny wooden cabin at the entrance of which I inscribed these words:

"*On the International Day of Peace - 1991 - this property was named the Margarita and Robert Muller Peace Park.*"

When President Reagan proposed that there should be yearly summit meetings between the leaders of the United States and of the USSR, my wife commented:

"They must be reading your books and speeches in the capitals."

*

What were my greatest loves? My wife, my children, my life, the Earth, humanity, the United Nations and God.

*

From a newsletter of the *American Association for Supervision and Curriculum Development*:

"160 curriculum developers from 14 countries met in Enschede, Netherlands, to begin shaping the definition of the knowledge all educated people should share on this planet. In our time, when the destruction of humanity could become a trump card in international contests, how much responsibility does curriculum have in fostering the connections among us? Plenty, answered Gordon Cawelti, Executive Director of the American Association. He urged conference participants to work toward a world core curriculum, with the long-term goal of assuring peaceful and cooperative existence among the human species on this planet. Cawelti endorsed UN Assistant Secretary-General Robert Muller's world curriculum, comprised of four elements:

1. **Our Planetary Home**, including an understanding of the universe, the biosphere and earth's ecosystem;
2. **The Human Family**, centering on the world population, human migration, geography, health, and living standards:
3. **Our Place in Time**, interpreting past, present, and future events;
4. **The Miracle of Human Life**, transmitting knowledge and attitudes needed for clear thinking and communication as well as good physical, mental, moral, and spiritual health".

I thank God and the UN who permitted me to develop this world curriculum.[20]

*

---

[20]   Taught for the first time in the Robert Muller School in Arlington, Texas, and since then in a growing number of other schools around the world.

I will never understand why peace is so difficult to achieve on this planet. How can there be people crazy enough to believe in wars, to endorse the military and to produce arms? I will never understand it. They have no justification. This planet and human life are too miraculous, too beautiful to permit anything but peace and cooperation of all humans.

*

During the fortieth anniversary year of the UN, I found on the nighttable of a Japanese hotel a Buddhist prayer book in which I read this story told by the Buddha:

"Once upon a time a father came home from a long trip. When he approached his dwelling, he saw that there was a fire in it. He shouted:
'Children, come out quickly, there is a fire in the house'.
But the children did not come out. So, he shouted:
'Children, I brought back beautiful toys for you. Please come out and see.'
And the children came out right away."

This story was an enlightenment to me. I discovered that I had been doing the same at the United Nations. Instead of telling people and governments about dangers and impending catastrophes, I told them to look at the beautiful things they could do together. Look at the marvelous toys and dreams which are expecting you. Look at the joys of achieving peace, justice and happiness for all. Why don't you play with your most beautiful toys, the United Nations and its specialized agencies, world conferences, world meetings and instruments?

*

I love foremost the world and humanity.
I have affection for my country and religion.
I consider this to be the right priority, the one laid down by
　God from the beginning.
No one on Earth has the right to turn this around.

*

My first commentary as Chancellor of the University for Peace was this:

"Generals inflamed their soldiers for victory. Their proclamations are often great, historic, literary texts. Who has ever inflamed peacemakers? Where are the great, historic literary, uplifting peace proclaimers? Not more than a handful, mostly the prophets and religious leaders. The University for Peace must join its inspiring voice to that of the religions and of the United Nations."

*

God has given me the urge and capacity to fight for underdogs. Today, the most downtrodden and defenseless underdogs are humanity and the Earth. This is why I am a fanatic of the United Nations which is the first universal instrument for the defense of underdogs.

*

I have made it a habit to think of the world and humanity from morning to evening and wherever I am. I even program myself to do it during my sleep. Try to do he same and you will be astonished by the results.

*

I am a specialist in impossibilities: I deal primarily with what seems impossible, in particular to make ours a peaceful, happy and beautiful planetary home.

I am a specialist in generalities. The universe, eternity, the earth, humanity, happiness, the soul, life, death, God, peace, justice, etc., I try to grasp it all. I am a forerunner of what more and more ordinary people will be in the next millennium.

*

I defended the UN when the Catholics attacked it during the McCarthy period. And I am a Catholic.

I defended the UN when colonialist France attacked it. And I am a Frenchman.

128

I defended the UN when General de Gaulle attacked it. And I was one of his underground fighters.

I defend the UN now that the Jews attack it. And some of my best friends are Jews.

I defend the UN now that the conservatives attack it. And I am politically a conservative.

Whoever might be next on the list, I will always defend the UN as long as humanity will not create a better world organization.

*

I will not be remembered for my work for the UN and for the University for Peace, but for the faith, hope, inspiration and happiness I gave to others through my writings, work, example and speeches.

All I attempted will not materialize during my lifetime, far from that. But all my attempts in the UN will sooner or later be recognized, cherished and implemented.

*

Have the vexations, attacks, criticisms and smears against the UN ever affected my faith? Of course not, for my faith is like a rock. And faith is unaffected even by death. Jesus won on the cross, not his detractors.

*

From the world's point of view, my presence and work at the UN for forty years was a blessing. From the point of view of the big powers, it was a nuisance. But in the long run, they will also find that it was a blessing, for without the UN, the nation-state sovereign system would have ended earlier and in a worse manner.

*

After a speech at the University for Peace, the Earth began to tremble. I said to the audience:

"The bad spirits seem to be mad at me."

A listener commented:

"On the contrary, they are applauding you."

After another speech, a woman said:

"While you spoke I saw a rainbow rise over the mountains. You were showing us the pot of gold at the end of it."

*

Oh God, what beautiful things I will be missing on this planet once I am dead! Please allow me to continue to work for it as a spirit, to show your children the pot of gold, and discover the holy grail.

*

A life is worthwhile only through the joys and happiness we give to others.

*   *
*

7

The UN and the People

People often complain that there are too many wars on this planet and that there will always be wars. They are unduly pessimistic. The planet has not seen a world war in the last forty years, while several could have broken out. My grandfather knew three wars, my father two, I one, and neither of my sons did military service. Regarding local wars, I once sat down and compared the world statistics on automobile accidents. The number of dead and injured people was several times greater than that of people killed or wounded in local wars. Yet, people complain more about wars than about automobile accidents.

*

So many people in the world are working for peace and the common good of humanity that national governments and their misbehavior are becoming impardonable obstacles to world progress. It is high time for the people to lead the leaders.

*

When you close your eyes forever on this beautiful planet, will you be able to say: I have done some good for the world and I leave it a little better than I found it?

*

A young man who heads an NGO with the UN, adopted this text by Dag Hammarskjöld as a guideline for his life:

"Working at the edge of the development of human society is to work on the brink of the unknown. Much of what is done will one day prove to have been of little avail. That is no excuse for the failure to act in accordance with our best understanding, in recognition of its limits but with faith in the ultimate result of the creative evolution in which it is our privilege to cooperate."

*

As a result of humankind's historic progress, we are asked to be good, hopeful, peaceful, concerned citizens towards:
- ourselves
- our family
- our profession
- our community
- our nation
- the environment

Plus towards these three vital categories:
- our planet
- humanity
- God, the universe and time.

*

Since ours is a complex, interdependent world, there is the need for a complex, interdependent citizenship. U Thant called it multiple allegiances to: oneself, family, the city, nation, profession, humanity, the Earth and to Heaven.

*

If the UN is as ineffective as people are led to believe in some countries, then those who are scared of it would not spend millions of dollars and mobilize so much brainpower to assail it. They would simply ignore it.

*

We are all for a peaceful, happier and better managed world. Why don't we all take an interest in the first universal organization ever created to do this? It is weak and ineffective, you will say, because you have been told so. First, this is only partly true and is to be expected at this juncture of our checkered history which has left us 179 sovereign nations. Second, even if it were true, it would merely increase your responsibility to force your government to make the UN more effective.

*

The first and foremost duty of every peacemaker is the support, strengthening and thorough knowledge of the UN.

*

If everyone cared for and loved the UN, it would do miracles.

*

The UN has only two things to fear: The ignorance and apathy of the people.

*

If you owe something to someone, if you work for a government, a firm, a group, or an institution, you may easily lose part of your freedom. You will be prejudiced by your allegiance. The more allegiant you are, the more you will be rewarded by your group and the less truthful you might be to the Earth and humanity.

The merit of the UN and of its agencies is that their servants take an oath of allegiance exclusively to humanity and to the world. They can judge therefore truthfully what is really good and bad for our planet and for the human race. This is why they deeply influence the course of human and Earth destiny.

You too, must make your pledge of allegiance to the world and to humanity. We all must be world servants.

*

People should always distinguish between the UN as an entity and the behavior of individual governments. The world organization should not be condemned **in toto** for the misbehavior of a few governments or leaders.

A body is not necessarily sick because of a few local wounds. Heal those wounds but do not give up the whole body. Yet this is how many people behave towards the UN. Their insistence on having a perfect UN instantly may lead to having no UN at all.

*

All of my work, writings, speeches, thoughts and actions have only one objective: to make the people better understand, love and support the United Nations, their first universal organization ever, and our best hope and chance for survival on this planet.

*

Until I knew U Thant I did not know what a wonderful man he was. Similarly most people do not know what a wonderful organization the United Nations is. Knowledge is the first step to understanding and respect. If you know your United Nations you will love it. Join your local United Nations Association. If there is none, create one.[21]

*

In every institution there is good and there is evil. The UN is not exempt from this rule. But why is it that the media of the western world are so overwhelmingly and passionately keen on what is wrong? For one good article, program or book about the UN there are at least ten on its failures and deficiencies. Why don't we read nice stories about the people who work at the UN, about their noble efforts and ideals, their hard work, progress and successes? Why not?

*

The UN is not responsible for the conflicts and lawlessness of this planet; national sovereignty is. We must face this reality. As long as the UN is not given the authority to enforce world law, this planet will remain in the present lawless and armed chaos it is now.

*

How many people in the United States protested when their government unilaterally declared that it would no longer recognize the jurisdiction of the International Court of Justice? The people of a country which made law and justice the cornerstone of their nation remained utterly silent.

*

---

[21]   Write to United Nations Association of the US, 485 Fifth Avenue, New York, NY. 10017-6104

As the optimist-in-residence at the UN I say to an optimist:
"Global institutions are our greatest chance to turn the tide."

To a pessimist I say:
"There is no alternative to global institutions in the world of today".

To a UN hater I say:
"Alright, I accept your criticisms. Let us then abolish the UN, but what would you create instead?"

*

If the people strongly supported the UN, governments could not say to me: "Mr. Muller, why should we do what your propose? Our people do not support the UN."

*

No other institution on Earth should be looked at with less prejudice than the UN. If viewed with prejudice, you will never see the true image of our planet and of humanity.

*

It is simplistic to condemn the UN for all of the evils on Earth when it is the weakest, most powerless political organization ever devised by humans.

*

The UN is a heroic organization: it tackles the most intractable problems of humanity: peace, justice, disarmament, human rights, racial equality, hunger, illiteracy, the environment, equality of the sexes, epidemics, drugs, violence, etc. As all heroes, it deserves at least some encouragement and love from the people.

*

Since the UN is dealing with the most difficult problems on Earth, do not encourage it to fail, but help it to succeed.

*

New views, even if they are right and timely, are called heresies and are bitterly fought by the opponents of change. Thus the UN is called a heresy by isolationists and is bitterly fought by them.

*

There is a *"UN We Believe"* organization.

The Baptists have adopted the motto: *"UN We Trust"*

We still need a:
- *"UN We know"*
- *"UN We understand"*
- *"UN We act"*
- *"UN We love"*

*

When the UN is attacked, I am consoled that it is better to be attacked than to be ignored.

*

Comment of a UN journalist:

"The situation is excellent for UN correspondents, because the international situation is getting worse."

*

Comment of a UN correspondent:

"Mr. Muller, we have it so good these days: there is Afghanistan, the war between Iran and Iraq, and lots of other troubles. I fear the moment when all this is settled. What will we do? Our bosses are likely to close our offices."

*

Many people look for hope and inspiration from the United Nations. However peace starts in your heart and mind, not in a meeting of the United Nations.

*

The people should never say: The UN is not good.
They should say: The UN is not good enough.

*

What would the UN be without governments? - An empty shell.
What would governments be without people? - Empty shells.

Therefore, in whose hands lies the fate of the UN? - In the hands of the people.

This is why the Charter starts with the words:

"We, the Peoples. . ."

*

Given the increase in the world population, the mounting pressure on resources and the danger that this planet might become unlivable, it is time to cleanse our lives of all that is harmful, wasteful and unnecessary. The suppression of national borders and the incredible duplication of national expenditures, especially of armaments are the first imperatives. But each citizen of this planet should also contribute asking himself or herself every day: what can I do for a better environment? Is what I do, buy and consume really indispensable?

*

People should spend their lives doing good and avoiding evil. Think for a moment of all the good you can do over a lifetime. It is incredible. We are indeed instruments of God on Earth. We are the greatest living tools of cosmic good. We are all servants of the UN, servants of the Earth, and servants of Humanity.

*

Most people look at the UN through national glasses, with national eyes, with national minds and with national hearts. No wonder they will never understand the UN. They are likely to die without having understood the true challenges of our time and the real meaning and potential of their first universal organization.

*

Every human on this Earth should be given once in his life the opportunity to work for another nation or for a world organization, international association or cause.

*

So many human dwellers of this planet say:
"I am proud of my country."

Too few say:
"I am proud of my planet, of my human family."

The United Nations is trying to bring about this indispensable change in attitude. But the process is slow, so terribly slow, and time is getting so short.

*

Have you done something for the UN of late? Have you ever done anything for it? If not, don't expect miracles from the UN and for it to be the savior of humanity and the planet.

*

I do not understand why people do not love the UN and make it the object of their concern and support. The United Nations and world unity must become the concerns of all people.

*

Dear Reader,

I can see you object very strongly and say:

"There is a world of difference between **You** and the UN, and **We** and the UN. You had the privilege of working in the UN for so many years. We have not. We will never be able to care for it as much as you do."

My answer:

"You do not have to work in your national government to care for your nation or even to be ready to kill and to be killed for it. Similarly, you do not need to work for the UN to care for the planet and your human family. Since you are so deeply programmed by your nation, I consider it my duty to convey to you my views and recommendations, for humanity's benefit."

*

The media have an immense responsibility. If they so desired, the UN could be better known, understood and hence more effective for the good of all.

*

The best-selling authors and film-makers of the world should take an interest in the UN and have their novels[22] and films unfold in the UN and/or deal with subjects of major world concern. This would help educate the people and perform a vital social role.

*

---

[22]   I made two attempts, writing a French novel *"Sima Mon Amour"*, which received a French literary award, and *"First Lady of the World"*, in which a woman becomes Secretary-General of the UN.

What can be your contribution to world peace?
To be a kind, peaceful and good person.

*

If you love peace and the world, please love the UN. The more you love the UN, the more courageously and enthusiastically its delegates and workers will labor for peace and a better world.

*

For the UN to succeed, it needs great impetus, enthusiasm and love from all five billion people of this planet.

*

A planet such as ours, infested with nuclear arms, is the supreme insult to God and to the cosmos. All conceivers, developers, producers, sellers and users of these arms will surely be condemned in the nether world. I would not like to be one of them for all of the power, glory and material gain in the world.

*

If you want to help God, the world and humanity, you must begin by believing that you are an instrument of God. If not, how can you expect to achieve anything?

*

Citizens have gained personal involvement in national affairs but not in world affairs. They have been kept away from them. They have not realized that they can be powerful international motivators who can substantially change "foreign" and world policies. International non-governmental organizations are the first to understand that. Join them and begin to create a true, vocal world democracy.

*

Has your government ratified the University for Peace created by the UN in Costa Rica? If not, write to your President to have it done. It is one of the most important projects of human evolution on Earth.

*

Sign your letters with "**yours in peace**" instead of "yours sincerely". Sincerely means "without wax", from the Latin "*sine cera*". Whenever a competition of sculptures took place in ancient Rome, inspectors examined the marble works to see if cracks had been covered with wax. If not, they declared the sculptures to be "*sine cera*" and therefore eligible for prizes. There is little reason to keep this antiquated letter ending. We must use one better suited to our needs and time.

*

Concentrate on the most difficult tasks. Do what the majority of people hesitate or do not want to do. Support the United Nations or one of its innumerable endeavors for peace and a better world. Humanity will thank you and you will be rewarded with untold happiness.

*

We need a new breed of men and women to make the world what it was always meant to be: One planet inhabited by one human family.

*

Oh people, I implore you, do not be impatient with the UN, or dismiss it and discourage its workers. Think of the difficulties you have with your own interest groups and countries. Do you think it is easy to mold 179 sovereign nations and five billion people into a community? It is one of the most difficult tasks on Earth. Please be patient with us, as patient as you are with the workers of a new profession. And above all, support us, do not throw stones at us, and pray for us.

*

The United Nations has many visitors but few supporters. We are still a curiosity, not a commitment.

*

The UN is really the organization of the down-trodden. It has no power, no riches, no warriors, no merchants on its side. It is the most noble attempt at world peace and justice ever in human history. Its power is essentially moral. Its survival and success therefore rest essentially in the hearts and support of the people. And it is those hearts and minds which the enemies of the UN are trying to poison. Beware, Oh people!

*

The UN is the most recent attempt in civilized history to find the rules of conduct, peace and happiness for the human race on Earth. Its success or failure will depend largely on the understanding of the people. If this attempt fails, it will not be the fault of governments alone, it will also be the fault of the people. The UN is in your hands.

*

To me the most incomprehensible thing on this planet is that people are ready to kill and be killed in the name of a nation, a religion or for material gain, and even accept medals and awards for these acts!

*

There is a seed of love for the UN in every human heart. Do not let it be stifled. Make it grow and you will become an instrument for a better world.

*

The UN works so hard for the peace, justice, health and happiness of the people of the world, and yet it receives so little recognition and encouragement.

*

Every human being can be a world servant, a servant of humanity, a servant of God and the universe, a helper of the United Nations. Remember:

"We, the Peoples. . ."
*

Arriving in Geneva, I was once received by a group of young people who drove me to my hotel. They asked me:

"How is it that you look so young and seem so enthusiastic and optimistic?"

My answer to them:

"It is because I work for the United Nations where I see that humans can succeed and work together. Like an artisan, I am happy because there is so much to do. If you want to feel like me, take an interest in the UN."

I give this advice to all young people of the world as well as to the elderly. I have observed that people working for UN associations and non-governmental organizations[23] get very old because they always have so much to do and they love it.

*

Paraphrasing John F. Kennedy:
People always ask;
"What does the UN do for me?"
They never ask;
"What do I do for the UN?"

*

If people could have for the world and humanity the same love they have today for their nation, it would be the biggest step ahead towards world peace.

*

Look at the United Nations and you will see a perfect image of humanity, of the world and of yourself.

*

After thousands of years of bloody history, we are lucky to have at long last a universal organization. It is only common sense for the people to welcome it, to rejoice at it, to support, nurture and strengthen the UN?

*

From a reader:
"I brought a friend along to visit the UN. She was thrilled by the 'light' shining from so many men and women dedicated to nurturing and preserving our human family. I myself, each time I visit the UN, I am moved to tears."
Pablo Casals too, cried every time he visited the UN.

*

My most fervent prayer is that the UN will grow into the hearts of every human being on Earth.

*

---

[23]   Non-governmental organizations - NGOs.

I will simply never understand the enmity and indifference of some people for the UN. It makes me doubt the sanity of the human race. Don't they understand how wrong and counter-productive they are?

*

If only all of the people on this planet could decide to do something for a better world. Most people give up and consider the world hopeless. As a result, it becomes hopeless.

*

If only the whole world would celebrate United Nations Day, on October 24, anniversary of the birth of the first universal organization. May all countries on Earth follow the example of several African countries which responded to the General Assembly's invitation and declared United Nations Day a holiday.

*

Each year on August 6, the anniversary of the Hiroshima bomb, many churches and temples around the world ring their bells.

It took an atom bomb to make humans feel together. Why not share also our feelings of joy? Why not ring the bells on October 24, birthday of the United Nations?

Humans are still too negative. We have been trained to be "against" something and not to be "for" something. Until we reverse this trend we will not succeed. We must be a positive, hopeful humanity.

*

I wish that all of the people of this world born on October 24, would also celebrate the birthday of the United Nations. They should call themselves children of the United Nations. There are about 13 million of them. They should learn about the United Nations and the family into which they were born.

*

There is one day in the year that should shine brighter than all national holidays:

24 October, United Nations Day.

*

I said to young advertisers:

"If you present well the UN to the people, getting their support for the world organization and forcing governments to abide by its rules, not only will you have done your job well, but you will have lived useful lives contributing to peace, further civilization and cosmic progress on this planet in its journey in the universe. And you will be recompensed with untold happiness."

*

From a Gallup poll taken on the occasion of the fortieth anniversary of the UN:

"Eighty percent of Americans are unable to name any agency of the United Nations Organization. The figure is even higher, at eighty six percent, among young adults 18 to 29 years old. Perhaps even more shocking is that sixty percent of college graduates are unable to name any agency."

Carbonated "soft-drinks" and hamburgers are better known in the world than this peace organization.

*

Everyone expects the UN to resolve all the conflicts on Earth. Have you asked yourself if you have resolved any conflicts within yourself or with others?

*

In a survey about the United Nations, one teacher from the US thought it was a territory where criminals from around the world were being kept! After the initial shock, I thought that such a territory was not such a bad idea after all. Quite a few candidates for such a place came to my mind.

*

Excerpts from letters sent by citizens of India to the UN on its fortieth anniversary:

"The UN is a plant that needs the support of its members and peoples to grow. When it has grown, its fruits will reach the entire world and achieve the miracle of peace, progress and prosperity for all."

"May I suggest a new name for the United Nations without abandoning its abbreviation: Universal Nation of Oneness.

Let us feel that **UNO** is not just an organization, but a single nation of everyone. Let each one on this Earth feel that he and she belongs to it."

"As there is no alternative to peace, there is no alternative to the United Nations."

*

Since U Thant was never shown a monument to unknown peacemakers, but only to unknown soldiers, it is high time to correct this situation: The more we will honor peacemakers, the less there will be unknown soldiers.

*

Idealistic and naive are those who do not believe in the UN. Check these words in a hundred years.

*

The life of each person, group and nation is part of a mysterious global journey. What we do together amounts to much more than what we do individually. Only time and the future will tell what our real influence was.

*

If only people knew how great the work of the UN is in so many fields! But few are educated about the UN, and the media report only what is bad or wrong in the glass house. There is a shattering distance between what the UN does and the cynicism and indifference of the people. In my view, the UN building should be redesigned in the form of a Cross.

*

A person who heard me speak wrote to me:
"When you are working in the UN, your life is entirely guided by it, but when you are working outside in unconnected and unrelated work, you don't even know that such a thing as the UN exists."

On the contrary, there is no work on this planet which is unrelated to the endeavors of the UN. It is one of the great tasks of educators and political leaders to build bridges between the people, their professions and the related global work of the United Nations and of its thirty-two specialized agencies.[24]   A better world is our common endeavor, from the individual to the top of the world. We must all fit into the great universal framework of our planet's evolution.   You can all join one of the international associations in your profession or field of interest.[25]

*

If I was young, I would create a world fundamentalist movement. The planet, humanity, the family and the individual would be our fundamental concerns, overriding any other interests.

*

The Vatican distributes to youth a "little blue book" by the Pope, contrasting with Mao Tse Tung's "little red book".
I have been doing the same for many years, distributing another "little blue book" containing the Charter of the United Nations.

*

A thirteen year old Brazilian girl won the national contest on the UN's fortieth anniversary with this sentence:

"The UN begins at home."

*

Anyone and everyone should celebrate the anniversaries and international days of the UN,[26] especially in the schools.

*

---

[24]   I list my proposals for education in my acceptance speech of the 1989 UNESCO Peace Education Prize. (*"Dialogues of Hope"*, pages 171-177 - 1990, World Happiness and Cooperation)

[25]   Consult your library for the *"Yearbook of International Associations"*, K.G. Saur, - Munchen, New York, London, Paris.

[26]   For a list see Appendix 3, or write to the UN Public Inquiries Unit, Room GA-57, United Nations, NY. 10017

To change the world we must support the UN with all of our heart.

*

Parents raise and nurture their children.
The UN is the child of humanity.
Should you therefore not be helping?

*

I was glad to get the Montessori schools accredited by the UN. The United Nations is the greatest Montessori school on Earth.

*

At the UN, many visitors bring us good ideas, a good heart, little projects, great projects, and their concern and love for the world and humanity.

I sometimes wonder what visitors are bringing to the Pentagon and military academies.

*

Many foreign students graduating in the United States and in other countries insist that their national flag or the United Nations flag be raised at the graduation ceremony. International students associations should promote this good practice.

*

I receive many new designs for world or planetary flags. I always reply that we have a world flag officially adopted by all nations, the United Nations flag. People should display it prominently with respect and love.

*

At a conference in Strasbourg I saw a remarkable display of flags. The French flag in the middle, the flag of Europe on the left and the UN flag on the right. Similar miniature flag arrangements were in front of all delegates to remind them they were French, European and World citizens.

This good example should be followed everywhere in the world.

*

I always ask that a United Nations flag be displayed when I speak to any group or at a university. If none is available, I bring one along with me as a gift.

Since I deliver about 180 speeches each year, this amounts to 180 UN flags displayed in front of many thousands of people.

In each of my autographed books, I affix a little gummed United Nations flag. This small gesture puts into circulation a few thousand additional United Nations flags.[27]

Dear reader, please help promote humanity's flag. In the 18th and 19th centuries the US flag was rarely seen anywhere in America. Only state flags were displayed. The same is true today with the UN flag.

*

I wish someone would create a world association for the promotion of the United Nations flag. On United Nations Day, I would like to see the whole world raise the blue United Nations flag. You can become an instrument of peace by displaying the United Nations flag on your home, your factory, your firm, your school, your hotel, your church, your car, your bicycle, and above all, in your heart.

*

We want to change the world, but sometimes are not ready to change ourselves. Think of all your faults. Make a list of them. It is only after you have changed them that you can begin to reform the world. Since we have our own faults it is natural that the world should have its faults also, multiplied and magnified by 5 billion people. If I consider my faults as being natural, should I not consider the faults of the world as being natural too?

*

It is not so much socialism and capitalism which we must fight, but militarism which infests almost all nations.

*

Rituals manifest a feeling of faith and togetherness. All religions understand this and incorporate rituals in their sacraments. Nations follow this example. Today we need world rituals to manifest our faith in humanity and in a better world. The United Nations has

---

[27]   See Appendix 3 for sources to order UN flags.

adopted many world celebrations and symbols which people should support.

*

Moses gathered sixty of his disciples to appoint them as prophets, but two of them did not show up. They were already out educating the people. Moses exclaimed:

"Oh how I wish that all the people of Israel follow their example and became prophets!"

I express the same wish for the 5 billion people of Earth. Become prophets of the UN, of peace and of a better world. The result will be no wars, armaments or militaries anymore.

*

The fortieth anniversary of the United Nations was the first world-wide celebration on this planet. A feeling of world togetherness and consciousness was created. The effects of this precedent will be long lasting. The fiftieth anniversary of the UN will be even better. The World Bimillennium will be even greater.

*

On the occasion of the fortieth anniversary of the UN, the *New York Times* published a series of positive articles about the UN. The headline of the series of articles read:

"The UN celebrates its 40th anniversary. Many types of humanitarian and peace-keeping operations being conducted around the world symbolize the essential work of the world organization."

When I expressed surprise at this unusually kind treatment of the UN by the *New York Times*, Abe Rosenthal one of the chief editors, answered:

"Well, we thought that it was about time to say a little hello to our neighbor."

*

We should not spend so much time defending the UN. All our strength, hearts and minds should be engaged to devise new dreams and efforts for a better world and to make the UN succeed.

*

Those who criticize the UN are anti-evolutionary, blind, self-serving people. Their souls will be parked in a special corral of the universe for having been retarding forces, true aberrations in the evolution and ascent of humanity. I pity UN haters and non-believers. Their friends in history were the protagonists of slavery, children's exploitation, women's discrimination, racism, and similar evils. The future will show how wrong and misguided they are.

*

Those remembered by humanity are people who gave their human brothers and sisters a sense of faith, hope, belief in life, elevation, beauty and pride to be human. Their recompense is normal:

Life and death are mysteries which engender fear in most people. Hence our gratitude to those who provide antidotes to that fear. The greatest of all, Jesus, gave us faith in eternal life and upgraded us as children of God.

*

People should understand that all the world's problems and solutions are essentially rooted within ourselves, be it love or hatred, greed or generosity, egotism or altruism, peace or violence, kindness or arrogance, joy or sadness. Each of us therefore is a basic factor and component of the world situation. If you want to do something for a better world, start with yourself and contribute to the world your love, generosity, altruism, kindness, peace, understanding, optimism and happiness. Radiate it all around you from morning to evening your entire life, and you will be one of the greatest peacemakers ever.

*

I cannot change the world, but I can change myself. And by changing myself I change the world.

*

Those in power program the people to believe they are powerless and unable to change the world. As a result, those in power remain powerful and the world does not change. Democracy, the exercise of the power of the people is not limited to elections every four or five years. Democracy is the daily exercise of power and communication, or networking with others. Networking is the new democracy.

*

As a very old man and delegate to the UN, the French human rights fighter and Nobel Prize winner, René Cassin, was known to spend his weekends in his hotel writing dozens of letters by hand advocating his cause. Returning to the French delegation on Monday mornings, he would send these letters asking people to act upon his ideas. I have followed his example and think more people should too.

*

If the Ford Foundation, the Rockefeller Foundation or any other foundation in the world convened people from around the globe in one place to study and confer on all the world's problems, issues, challenges, discoveries, plans and dreams, they would receive worldwide acclaim. Well, this is exactly what the United Nations and its specialized agencies do, but rarely is the UN congratulated or offered financial support. On the contrary, we are criticized, placed on the defensive, harassed by investigating committees, accused of bureaucracy and of spending too much.

People may think it is wonderful to work for the United Nations, but there are days when I feel a dog's life is better.

*

One of my readers called me and expressed concern at the increase of militarism in the world and stepped up attacks aimed at the United Nations. I said to her that I had just returned from Costa Rica where I had found the secret of peace: the outlawing of the military.

Costa Rica is the only peaceful, democratic country in Central America. If tomorrow Costa Rica introduced an army, the military would want their budget increased every year. To effect their claims the military would predict, imagine or stage all kinds of trouble to prove their need for more resources. Therefore the suppression of the military is the secret.

In response, she told me the following anecdote:

"The other day I said to my five-year old boy that the military in El Salvador were killing children.

My son answered:

'They are stupid, because if they want to be liked by their people, they should not kill children. They should be nice.'

That is a good answer, son. Perhaps when you are grown-up you will work for peace.

'Oh no', answered my boy, 'Because then the military will kill me'."

*

People often ask me:

"How can you be so optimistic? Aren't you frustrated and ready to give up?"

I answer:

"No, because I feel like a doctor, I do my very best and I always take the view, as does a doctor or surgeon, that I can heal or at least help the patient. If I fail, I say to myself; 'I did my best, and I learned something which might help next time.' I would hate to be operated on by a pessimistic surgeon who doubted his ability to succeed. The same is true with world servants."

*

At the exit of a zoo in India, there is a curtain with this sign above it, asking:

"Which is the most cruel animal on Earth?"

Visitors draw the curtain and see their own face reflected in a mirror. We should have a similar device at the exit of the United Nations.

*

Dag Hammarskjöld and a UN journalist were walking back to their offices after a press conference by the Secretary-General. The journalist commented sadly:

"Isn't it a shame that the UN is not taken more seriously. Several newspapers are closing their offices at the UN. The questions put to you were so critical, so unfair. Several non-governmental organizations are also giving up."

Dag Hammarskjöld stopped walking, looked sternly at the journalist and said:

"I do not see any problem. You and I remain, and as long as there is one person on Earth who believes and acts for the right course, there is no reason to despair."

*

Each human wants to have a good conscience but seldom does one ask what he or she can do for a better world. This is why the question of peace is left to the United Nations without much public interest or support for the organization. I pity those who at their death have no answer to God's question:

"What have you done for peace and a better world?"

*

I spent most of my adult life working for the most difficult cause on Earth - the United Nations. I am glad I did.

In my retirement I now am engaged in an even more difficult task - the UN University for Peace in Costa Rica.

May God and my friends help me.

*

Do not be afraid to have a utopian idea, dream or vision for the world. Usually it is these dreams that work. Remember what Arthur Schopenhauer said:

"All truth passes through three stages:

First it is ridiculed;
Second it is violently opposed;
Third it is accepted as self-evident."

*

Everyone can be a diplomat, a peacemaker, an artisan of a better world, even children and senior citizens. I could give many examples. I myself am a retired one-dollar-a-year Chancellor of the University for Peace. A retired railroad man, Irving Sarnoff, has created an association of friends of the United Nations. Another friend, former Ambassador John McDonald, has created an Institute for Multi-Track Diplomacy, which includes peoples' diplomacy.

Learn from them, follow their examples, do something for heaven's sake and remember the Chinese saying:

"When the people lead, the leaders will follow."

*

"Never doubt that a small group of thoughtful, committed citizens can change the world. Indeed it is the only thing that ever has."

Margaret Mead

*

"Think peace   -   and there will be peace.
Believe in peace   -   and you will be rewarded by peace.
Look for peace   -   and you will find peace.
Prepare for peace   -   and you will receive peace.
Expect peace   -   and you will be treated in peace.
Live in peace   -   and you will inspire peace.
Honor peace   -   and you will be blessed with peace.
Think peace   -   and there will be peace."

Edward M. Gilman

There will be no peace in the world if there is no peace in you.

*   *
*

Decide to Be Peaceful

Decide to be peaceful
Render others peaceful
Be a model of peace
Irradiate your peace
Love passionately the peace
of our beautiful planet
Do not listen to the warmongers
     hateseeders and powerseekers
Dream always of a peaceful
     warless, disarmed world
Think always of a peaceful world
Work always for a peaceful world
Switch on and keep on, in yourself
     the peace buttons
     those marked love,
     serenity, happiness, truth,
     kindness, friendliness,
     understanding and tolerance
Pray and thank God everyday for peace
Pray for the United Nations
     and all peacemakers
Pray for the leaders of nations
     who hold the peace of the world
     in their hands
Pray God to let our planet at long last
     become the Planet of Peace
And sing in unison with all humanity
     "Let there be peace on Earth
     And let it begin with me."

Decide to Network

Decide to network
Use every letter you write
Every conversation you have
Every meeting you attend
To express your fundamental
    beliefs and dreams
Affirm to others
    the vision of the world you want
Network through thought
Network through action
Network through love
Network through the spirit
You are the center of a network
You are the center of the world
You are a free, immensely powerful
    source of life and goodness
Affirm it
Spread it
Radiate it
Think day and night about it
And you will see a miracle happen:
    the greatness of your own life
In a world of big powers, media
    and monopolies
But of five billion individuals
Networking is the new freedom
    the new democracy
    a new form of happiness

8

The UN and Planetary Democratic Government

I once asked my son François what grade he would give humanity for the way our planet was being managed.

He answered; "I would give humans a triple "D": **Dumb, Dangerous and Disastrous**".

This encouraged me to express a similar view in a preface I wrote for the book "*Planethood*" by Ken Keyes and Ben Ferencz. This book raises, in effect, the following fundamental question:

"What would be the fate of the United States if each of its fifty states were sovereign, possessed an army, a President, a Supreme Court, a State Department, a CIA, a national hymn, a national flag, national days, and the exclusive power to levy taxes on its citizens? What if the United States government were no more than a United Nations without sovereignty, without legislative, executive, judicial, and fiscal powers, unable to make decisions and laws, but only recommendations and exhortations? You would exclaim: 'What an indescribable mess it would be!' Well, this is exactly the state of your planet torn up into 175 pieces!"[28]

*

[28]   "*PlanetHood*", second edition.   Love Line Books - 790 Commercial Avenue, Coos Bay, Oregon   97420

We live on the most ridiculously sliced up planet in the universe! If we discovered another planet divided politically like ours, we would laugh.

*

National democracy, **yes**.
World democracy, **no**.
Why?

*

In 1932 Einstein, having given up hope that humanity would find the answer to war and peace, turned to Freud and asked him if he had the answer. Freud wrote the following to him:

"Human instincts are of two kinds: those that conserve and unify, which we call 'erotic' (in the meaning Plato gives in his Symposium); and second, the instincts to destroy and kill, which we assimilate as the aggressive or destructive instincts. These are, as you perceive, the well-known opposites, love and hate, transformed into theoretical entities; they are, perhaps, another aspect of those eternal polarities, attraction and repulsion, which fall within your province."

And he concluded that peace and non-violence can only be achieved by "developing the love instincts" and by "the transfer of power to a larger combination, founded on the community of sentiments linking up its members." He therefore held the League of Nations to be a unique and hopeful development in human evolution:

"We would be taking a very shortsighted view of the League of Nations were we to ignore the fact that here is an experiment the like of which has rarely - never before on such a scale -been attempted in the course of history. It is an attempt to acquire the authority (in other words, coercive influence) which hitherto reposed exclusively in the possession of power, by calling into play certain idealistic attitudes of mind, including ties of sentiment or identification between the members of the group as opposed to violent compulsion."

In this answer lays the key to the fate of the human race: love for the planet and for all humanity; and world democratic government.

*

During the fortieth anniversary of the UN, a group of Alsatian children visited the UN. After the speech I gave them in the Dag Hammarskjöld auditorium, a little boy asked me this question:

"Why doesn't the UN eliminate all borders?"

I had no good answer, except to say that Alsatian-Lorrainers were the first to try to eliminate borders in Europe, that they succeeded, and that we will also succeed for the rest of the world.

*

In 1989, in my acceptance speech of the Peace Education Prize of UNESCO, I expressed the hope that I would be present in my home-town of Sarreguemines in Alsace-Lorraine to see the border between France and Germany dismantled once and forever in 1993. I hated this border during my entire youth, seeing it from my window and being constantly reminded of the division and misery it created for my family and for so many people.

*

How can I respect nationalism, when it caused my poor grandfather to have five successive nationalities in his lifetime without leaving his village, my father to be first a German soldier and then a French soldier, and myself to be in the French underground, while my cousins wore French and German uniforms?

I hate not only war, but also artificial national borders and sovereignty. This is my right. This is my freedom.

*

We must start independence movements for the Earth and humanity. Why should there be national borders? Rivers, mountains, fields and humans existed long before artificial nations and borders.

*

For the first time since 1987, my new French passport has the title:

European Community
- France -

I pray that soon the passports of my children and grandchildren will bear the title: **United Nations** or **World Community** and below it the name of their country.

*

The present political system of this planet obscures and distorts the real relationships that must prevail between humans, the Earth, the universe, God and eternity. Ours is probably one of the most primitive political systems in the cosmos. The United Nations is a first attempt at a new direction.

*

At this stage of our evolution we should be ready for world democratic government, for world democratic federalism or at least for proper world management. Alas, the world is not even mentally and sentimentally ready for the weak United Nations. The time has come to think of a bold new political system. Today we need a planetary democratic government and we will certainly have one within the next twenty to thirty years. The UN system is an unprecedented attempt by humanity at self organization. It is a first response to the fundamental urge of humanity to live in peace and to organize itself properly on this planet. It merits more recognition.

*

Humans are basically insecure. This is why they want security: family security, job security, social security and national security. Why not go one step further and give them world security, the security not to be killed in a war or to vanish in an environmental disaster? Why stop at national security? Aren't we living in the worst insecurity of all: planetary insecurity?

*

In our modern, rapidly changing times, the airports of planet Earth are usually rebuilt every ten years. Hospitals are modernized every few years. Strangely enough, the most important traffic and healing center on Earth, the United Nations, has not been remodeled once in forty years! There is something wrong with that.

*

Strangely, the UN cannot guarantee what it was established for, namely peace. Why? Because it is based entirely on the goodwill of nations and has no enforcement power. It is as if for a large city one would say: there is no need for law and order, all that people have to do is to be nice to each other.

The nation-state has contributed much to the advancement of social justice. Law protects, while unlawfulness gives a free hand to the rich and powerful. Therefore we need a world-state with the same function as the nation-state, but world-wide. The rich and powerful invade and rule the world, because there is no world law, no world-state, only a free-for-all jungle for the powerful and rich.

*

If nations perish, it is the big powers which will have been responsible for letting the nation-state system become inoperable, and for not having strengthened the UN as a means for proper democratic world governance.

*

Suppose there will be no nuclear war that will destroy this planet. Then try to think what life will be on this planet in one hundred, one thousand or in two thousand years. You will conclude that the present political "system" and endless economic destruction of this planet cannot survive for long.

*

While so much has been accomplished by science and technology, the only three worthwhile, imaginative achievements in the political field during the last forty years are: the UN, the Marshall Plan, and the European Community. There is an insufficient list of accomplishments for a world beset with a host of mounting global problems.

*

The UN is a much better forum for the democratic management of world relations in contrast to letting national interests use force and greed rule the planet. The UN is still very new at it. The tasks before this forum have never been attempted before. A new world political system must sooner or later be devised with effective legislative, executive and judicial powers.

*

When Victor Hugo declared that humanity needed a United States of the World, his friends thought that he had gone mad.

Well, today, we have a universal United Nations which is undoubtedly the first step towards a United States of the world.

*

Nation-states are too big to handle local problems and too small to handle global problems.

*

Increacing diversity is the rule of the universe. No two human beings, animals, insects or plants will ever be exactly the same in the entire universe and stream of time. Yet all atoms, cells, insects, plants, animals and human beings are parts of vast families of basically similar structures, characteristices and functions. Unity in diversity must be the central rule of a planetary society if we do not wish to run counter to biological evolution.

*

We humans consider ourselves to be the most advanced, intelligent species on Earth since we are endowed with the largest brains for our body size. However, bees and ants with minuscule brains are able to build societies far more orderly and cleaner than ours.

*

The world is a tremendous, interdependent reality. You can see it and feel it. The world wants to be cared for properly. Yet you are ready to let yourself be killed for limited, intangible, very recent, ever changing, self-promoting, artificial mortal entities called nations. Scores of nations, empires, kingdoms, republics and states have vanished during the millennia. History is a vast cemetery of nations, but the planet and its people are still here. When will we at long last recognize this glaring reality and give up the building of and support for doomed nations?

*

People die and nation-states persist.
Question:
For how long must newcomers be born into one of the 179 national partitions of this planet instead of into the global house and single human family?
Answer:
For as long as there are the military and arms manufacturers. Every nation should follow the wise example of Costa Rica and outlaw the military and armaments by Constitution.

*

When it comes to world government, it seems that all nations of Earth are sitting on the brains of their citizens, preventing them from even thinking about it!

*

Even if you don't want world government, the UN needs to be supported. You should request that the UN be strengthened to make its present mandates and functions work satisfactorily.

*

We should read once again the works of Simon Bolivar, Andres Bello and the great universal thinkers of the 18th and 19th century. They are true inspirations for world government.

*

Fundamentally, humans are perceptive, creative cosmic units of the universe's evolution on the planet we call Earth. To exercise their function correctly, people must be educated. Correct Global education and information, and the elimination of miseducation and misinformation, are fundamental prerequisites of democracy.

*

The UN is merely one approach among others of world cooperation and planetary management. Infinitely better methods should be designed and planned. There should be no taboos against planetary democracy, planetary federation, a United States of the planet and a planetary community.

*

Nationalism is to nations what egotism is to individuals, but much worse. Oppressive acts and propaganda are justified by the "reason of state". Rarely are nations brought before tribunals and punished as are individuals. National "sovereignty" often means impunity and tyranny.

*

Why the "interest of nations", the "reason of state"?
What about the "interest of humanity", the "reason of the Earth"?

*

It is a strange planet indeed where some are preparing for star wars while others wake up every morning in a war for daily food, water, wood and survival. Yes, it is an appallingly managed planet, unworthy of a place of honor in the universe. Our political leaders should feel ashamed down to the marrow of their bones. They should collectively resign.

*

Why should we wait for another world war to devise a better planetary system than the UN? Let us be sensible and either improve the UN or create a better world organization right away.

*

We discount world government as utopian because it is an unknown, and as long as we continue to discount it, it will remain an unknown and utopian.

*

Through multinational corporations, globalism is monopolized by the big powers and by private business. This is one more reason for a world democratic government.

*

Nations will not disarm, because the defense of their citizens is the principal justification for their existence. If you really want disarmament on this planet, you must abolish sovereign nations or reduce their sovereignty.

*

It is unbelievable that states, leaders and governments have not realized that we have entered a new period of history in which one global problem after the other will face humanity and will require proper world management and an entirely new political system.

*

I am glad that Claudine Brelet, my co-author of *"Planet of United Nations"*, is teaching a course of planetics instead of politics, (from "polis" - the city), at the Sorbonne in Paris.

*

Armaments are not a mistake in the present political context. But they are a phenomenal danger and waste in the new political

order needed for this planet. To work on a new political system will
be the fastest way to disarmament.

*

I believe the time has come for people to demand the withdrawal of the "taxing" and "borrowing" authority of national governments
and to give that authority to a democratically elected world government in the interest of the planet and humanity. Otherwise, nations
will continue to abuse their artificial sovereignty and they will bring
this planet to an end.

*

I will cease defending the UN only when I am offered a better
world institution. Would a surgeon give up the use of his imperfect
scalpel before he is offered a better tool?
Once the scalpel has been replaced, I would put the old one
aside with gratitude, and give all my heart to the new one.
What we must really care for is the health and well-being of our
good Earth and humanity, and devise the best instruments for that.

*

I would not even insist on seeing a different world order, or a
radical change in politics, or a world government. I would be quite
happy if nations would at least follow faithfully the UN Charter and
its treaties. Then we would have the beginning of an orderly, warless
society. One could start to build a coherent and better world society
and make further progress in human evolution. We are losing
precious time with the current misbehavior of nations.

*

The great political thinkers of our time are badly failing in their
responsibilities. They pay no attention to the ways in which this
planet should be managed. They pay even less attention to the first
school of planetary management: the United Nations and its
agencies. They discuss instead the "*balance of power*" and the endless
byzantine intricacies of "*foreign*" or international relations and
diplomacy. They should be ashamed of themselves.

*

A nation could not survive if it lost all of its people: it would
merely be an empty shell. But throughout history, billions of people

have survived the loss of their nation. Why then so much fuss about nations? Because they need that fuss to exist and to survive.

*

Communism is not funny.

Capitalism is not much funnier.

Why don't these two outdated, nineteen century regimes each give up their pretense at perfection and give a chance to a new world order, an up-to-date, modern one which is responsive to the real needs of the planet and of humanity?

*

The ozone layer of Earth's atmosphere is in danger. Europe implemented the recomendations of the UN convention concluded in Montreal in 1987 and even exceeded its requirements. But the US did not implement this convention. Why? Because it is sovereign. The UN prohibited driftnet fishing in the oceans. Japan continued to use driftnets. Why don't people rebel against their governments? And we call this an orderly planet? We are kidding ourselves.[29]

*

Do not call them nations anymore but planetary partitions: the French partition, the US partition, the Russian partition, the Chinese partition or provinces.

After the U.S. civil war, the heads of the confederate states became governors under the new federal US constitution. Today's "heads of state" should become governors or "trustees" of nations.

*

Oh, heads of state, why do you want to be great for only one of the 179 political partitions of this planet? Don't you want to be great in the eyes of the whole world, humanity and posterity? Don't you want to participate in the fashioning of a better world?

*

---

[29]   In February 1992, when a hole in the ozono layer developed above the United States, President Bush implemented the convention. Japan has now also given up the use of drift nets under public pressure. Nature and people seem to be better governors than governments.

It is absolutely urgent for heads of state to begin discussing how this planet should be governed and managed for its own sake and for the benefit of all humanity.

There should be a world organ for heads of states to meet, to talk, to study and to work together.[30] The present non-system in which each head of state sits in his or her capital like a feudal lord is unworthy of this beautiful planet. This system should be condemned loudly by the people.

*

My prayer to God: Oh God, save us from nations.

*

George Washington, in his will, left part of his inheritance for the creation of a national university. States were so opposed to his all-American views, that it was never created. We are luckier at the UN: there exist today a UN University, a supranational University for Peace, an International Maritime University and a World Institute for training in nuclear physics. May this novel trend spread to many more fields.

*

The US abandoned its support for UN after having engaged all other nations to participate in it for over forty years. The main complaint of the US:

Taxation without representation - the US pays 25% of the UN budget and has only one vote.

My answer: let us plan for a world federal government, patterned on the US constitution, which would give each adult human being a vote and each State a number of seats in a World House of Representatives and a World Senate. The US being the most advanced democracy on Earth should offer humanity a bold new political system for a free world democracy.

*

---

[30]   In January of 1992, for the first time in forty-seven years, the UN Security Council met at the heads of state level. Bravo! Also to be congratulated are Mr. Ingvar Carlson, former Prime Minister of Sweden, for his "Stockholm Initiative" which tackles the subject of world governance, and the Club of Rome for its project on governance for the 21st century.

To be a head of state for the glory of the title means little.

To be a good head of state, philosopher, peacemaker, world statesperson, a lover of people and the planet means much.

*

If it is not impossible to visualize that each person on this Earth plays a useful role in an institution or group, than it is not impossible to visualize that each person has a useful role to play in the world society?   Each person and group would then be validated as a coworker and contributor to human progress.

The UN represents this ideal for the relations between nations, but alas only the small and powerless countries understand that role. Each big power sees itself as the ultimate entity that should rule the world.   This is one of the main causes of our problems.

*

Most people of this Earth believe that they are powerless to change anything politically.   Democracy is limited to voting once every four or five years.   The study and improvement of democracy are a most fundamental subject of this last decade of our Millennium: perfection of democracy at the level of the individual through objective information and right education; world democracy beyond the borders of nations on the principle of one person, one vote. Individuals are the basic living perceptive units of our planet.   They must be educated, prepared and well informed to exercise this role properly without interference of power, wealth, advertisement, psychological, national or religious programming.   All living humans on this planet must be made global citizens, children of the Earth, instruments of God and of the universe.

*

Human history is paved with prejudices.   At one point there were good slaves and bad slaves; but slavery was good.   The pronouncements of St. Thomas of Aquinas and St Augustine on the inferiority of woman are appalling in today's world.

The question is now: what are our current prejudices which we accept and do not dare to challenge and which will look like horrors in times to come?   These include the infallibility of religion, the sovereignty of nations, the "reason of state" which allows nations to kill humans and to maintain horrendous armaments and armies. There are many others.

It is the role of the UN to uncover, denounce and fight these prejudices.

*

It would be an unforgivable blemish of our time, if this century and millennium passed without the establishment of a world constitutional Assembly to found a proper world democratic government for this planet.

*

I entered the UN thirty-eight years ago with an essay on world government. I leave it with the same conviction, stronger than ever, that world peace and disarmament will be possible only with world democratic government.

One should always remain truthful to the dream of one's youth. I must devote the rest of my life to the advocacy of a planetary democracy.

*   *
*

9

The UN and Spirituality

"The third millennium will be spiritual or there will be no third millennium."

André Malraux

*

It is not the United Nations, it is not even governments who are responsible for the current disorder in the world. It is the lack of spirituality, of respect for God and His miraculous Creation. There is so little spirituality in the world that I am surprised that there is not more chaos, conflict and sinning.

*

In the entire history of humankind, with the exception of a few great spiritual prophets, there has never been an attempt to see humanity governed by cosmic, divine, universal laws. The question of governing the whole human race has never arisen so far. And even today, its necessity is ignored by most political leaders.

*

What humanity needs most at this time is an active, dynamic, world-wide spiritual democracy. Like-minded people should work together for what they really, deeply believe as sensitive cosmic units meant to help the universe succeed in its cosmic experiment on this planet.

*

What is the craziest thought on Earth? The belief that we were created for ourselves, that our marvelous body and mind belong to us for no other reason than our enjoyment and exploitation of the Earth. Who would ever take such pains to create a being for no other purpose?

No, it cannot be. We were created for an infinitely higher purpose: probably to help God make this planet an evolutionary miracle in the universe.

*

Nowadays the skyscrapers are dwarfing the cathedrals. So let us make the whole planet a cathedral and we will have dwarfed the skyscrapers.

*

What the world needs most is architects of the Planet of God.

*

Our planet is **unique** as is any heavenly body in the universe. Even if there should be other inhabited planets, ours would be unique due to its specific conditions and evolution in a particular solar system.

But our planet is not **isolated**, it is not outside heaven, it is **in** heaven, it is part of it. We must therefore turn to the cosmos and to its laws, wisdom and "intelligence" for guidance. The UN must therefore become a cosmic, spiritual organization. Its tall building is a cosmic antenna, capturing the messages from the universe. What a great, fascinating story we are living!

*

Please, Oh God, wake up the leaders of nations to the greatness of this planet and of the human race. Make them understand their sacred, cosmic responsibility.

*

Politics should become a sacred function, the most holy, moral, ethical office on Earth. Like Robert Schuman, the father of the European Community, every political leader should be worthy of a process of canonization.

*

A little boy from the Robert Muller school in Texas, which teaches the universal framework of the UN, came home and said to his mother:

"Mommy, did you know that we are living in the heavens?"
This multi-billion year-old reality must become the consciousness of all people, especially of the leaders.

*

One thing I will never believe: That God or the universe took all the pain to create us in order to make money and to flood ourselves with material possessions.

*

The UN is still a predominantly secular organization. Its Secretary General is often assimilated to a secular Pope. It is the duty of all spiritual people to proclaim the necessity of a spiritual United Nations. This is particularly true of those nations whose spiritual beliefs have not yet been eroded by material secularism.

*

The UN must be the mother and teacher - *mater and magister* - of the peoples of the world, concerned not only with the fullness of their lives, but also with their soul. The UN will become the world's common religion, a universal spirituality of which existing religions will be diverse cultural members and manifestations.

*

The UN needs to be enriched by spiritual leaders, mystics, philosophers and sages, i.e. people with a total view of our place and journey in the universe and in time.

*

For Buddhists, Catholics, Jews and Muslims there is no distinction between life and spirituality. Why does not any of their delegates to the UN proclaim that? Why leave the world forum only to politicians, intellectuals, diplomats, rationalists and atheists? Delegates should all be inspired by the shining spiritual examples of Secretaries-Generals Dag Hammarskjöld and U Thant.

*

"The United Nations is something that the Creator, the author of all good, at every moment cherishes. No human force will ever be able to destroy the United Nations, for the United Nations is not a mere building or a mere idea; it is not a man-made creation. The United Nations is the vision-light of the Absolute Supreme, which is slowly, steadily and unerringly illumining the ignorance, the night of our human life. The divine success and supreme progress of the United Nations is bound to become a reality. At his choice hour, the Absolute Supreme will ring His own victory-bell here on Earth through the loving and serving heart of the United Nations."

Sri Chinmoy
Director of the UN Meditation Group
*

UN delegates and staff members should read the prophecies and deep spiritual insights of the United Nations' Guru, Sri Chinmoy. The young people who are looking to oriental sages and spiritual seers for enlightenment should also turn to him who has come from India to interpret the spiritual journey of the United Nations.[31]

*

In a first phase of its history, after the cataclysms of World War II, the UN naturally concentrated its efforts on the material needs of the world's people: reconstruction, avoidance of wars, economic development, health and sanitation, prevention of early death of children, longevity, avoidance of hunger and poverty, eradication of epidemics, literacy and education. This was the UN's first spirituality: the spirituality of the good Samaritan, help to the needy and not a discussion of the existence of God or the merit of religions. "Primum vivere deinde philosophari" - "First comes life, then philosophy", as the Latins said.

But soon this phase was transcended into a vaster canvas of world ethics and morality: the philosophy of human rights, of moral

---

[31]   See the many bulletins and books containing his interpretations, visions and prophecies published by the UN Meditation Group. Also see my book, *"Dialogues of Hope"*, (1990, World Happiness and Cooperation).

behavior, the need for codes of conduct for nations and multinational business, the immorality of nuclear arms, the ethics of the Earth, nature and all forms of life.

While none of these two phases has been completed world-wide, far from it, a new phase is on the horizon: the spiritual, universal or cosmic phase, our transcendence into the higher, perhaps ultimate attempt at full comprehension of our Earthly home and of all life on it. It will mean the recognition of planet Earth and of life, especially human life as evolutionary cosmic phenomena; the search of what the cosmos or God has in mind for us; the proper education, information and fulfillment of humans admitted to the miracle of life; our peace,harmony, union and cooperation with each other, with the Earth, with other life forms, with the heavens, with the past, present and future in the eternal stream of time; and the right rules of conduct and institutions to make this planet a showcase in the universe, a cosmic success.

*

"A new spiritual pyramid must be erected on the high intellectual platform that has already been built by the United Nations."

Rudolf Schneider
"Planetary Synthesis"

*

How many people in the world know that since 1946 every opening and closing of the yearly General Assembly of the UN took place with a minute of silence for prayer or meditation? That a Meditation Room was created in the UN, inspiring the creation of a Meditation Room in the US Congress, at the Council of Europe in Strasbourg and recently in the new building of the Australian Parliament? All the world's people should pray or meditate with their delegates on the third Tuesday of September, the day of the opening of the General Assembly, The International Day of Peace.

*

Through its pioneer work and early warnings on the environment, culminating in the UNCED II in Rio de Janeiro, the largest world conference ever in all human history, the UN has made an important contribution to the religiosity or spirituality of this planet:

respect for the Creation of God, for the sacredness of this planet, for its uniqueness in the cosmos, for the sanctity of all life on it.

*

To help other human beings or causes or institutions which are fostering peace and human progress is a spiritual task: who does so fulfills the will of God. It is not merely charity or altruism or self-interest. It is fulfilling a cosmic function, the role of a good cell in the total body of humanity. To support the United Nations is therefore a spiritual act. Pope Paul VI and Pope John Paul II said it clearly when they visited the United Nations.

*

A Catholic sister once explained to me why I had become a spiritual person at the UN:

"You were at the crossroads of all nations, at a center of the universal. You discovered that, you lived it and you became a universal, spiritual being. You had been cut from this source by your previous education and more limited interests."

This remark could be valid for every human being. Perhaps the ultimate role of the United Nations will be to transform all humans into universal spiritual beings.

*

There comes a day in the UN when one wakes up and asks these fundamental questions:

"What is it all about? What are we humans trying to do? What is the mystery of life in the vast universe and eternity? Why are we here? Why am I on this Earth? What is expected of me?"

On that day one becomes a spiritual person.

*

As a little boy I was a deeply spiritual being. I considered life, the heavens and our beautiful Earth to be divine. Then society, education and World War II severed me from my beliefs. I became a lawyer, an economist, a rationalist, an intellectual. I owe it to the UN, particularly to Secretaries-General Hammarskjöld and U Thant to have made me again a spiritual being.

*

I should have called my book, *"New Genesis, Shaping a Global Spirituality"*, *"United Nations, The Birth of a Global Soul"*.

*

Dag Hammarskjöld entered the UN as a high-level economist and government servant. At the UN he became a world servant and ended as one of the greatest mystics of our time. The word God never appeared in his " *Markings* " until he joined the UN. Then they became a constant dialogue with God. After his death, on his night-table his colleagues found the book of a mystic: " *Thomas A. Kempis, The Imitation of Christ.*"

*

Toward the end of his mandate Dag Hammarskjöld declared:
"I see no hope for permanent world peace. We have tried and failed miserably. Unless the world has a spiritual rebirth, civilization is doomed."

*

U Thant joined the UN as a deeply spiritual being, fully living his Buddhist faith. He lived the UN spiritually every single day. He left the UN with this spiritual message to the staff.

"... I have certain priorities in regard to virtues and human values. An ideal man, an ideal woman, is one who is endowed with four attributes, four qualities - physical, intellectual, moral and spiritual qualities. Of course it is very rare to find a human being who is endowed with all these qualities but, as far as priorities are concerned, I would attach greater importance to intellectual qualities over physical qualities. I would attach still greater importance to moral qualities over intellectual qualities. It is far from my intention to denigrate intellectualism, but I would attach greater importance to moral qualities or moral virtues - moral qualities like love, compassion, understanding, tolerance, the philosophy of, 'live and let live', the ability to understand the other person's point of view, which are the key to all great religions. And above all I would attach the greatest importance to spiritual values, spiritual qualities. I deliberately avoid using the term 'religion.' I have in mind the spiritual virtues, faith in oneself, the

purity of one's inner self which to me is the greatest virtue of
all. With this approach, with this philosophy, with this concept
alone, we will be able to fashion the kind of society we want,
the society which was envisaged by the founding fathers of the
United Nations."

*

U Thant could not understand that we westerners separate so
easily spirituality from life and leave it to a church service on Sunday.
For him his entire life, from morning to evening, was a spiritual
communion with the universe, with the Earth and humanity, even and
especially in the midst of a crisis or a difficult negotiation.[32]

*

When Secretary-General Javier Perez de Cuellar took up his
functions, his first visit was to the UN Meditation Room to ask for
God's blessings. He also replaced the national holidays granted to
the UN staff, by Holy Friday before Easter. He declared that the UN
should become a "holy family of nations".

*

On 15 September, 1993, the annual International Day of Peace,
Thanksgiving Square in Dallas will convene a Continental Convention
of the Spirit to seek God's guidance for the next 500 years of the
Americas and of the world. Since the Iroquois make their decisions
thinking of the seventh generation, I suggested that they should be
invited. Seven generations mean today seven times seventy-five years,
or 525 years.

*

Hopefully the second World Parliament of Religions in Chicago
in 1993 will create a World Spiritual Agency to be associated with the
United Nations and help it enhance its spiritual dimension.

*

---

[32]   For U Thant"s spiritual approach to world affairs, see the
chapter, How I conceived my Role, in his memoirs, "The View from
the UN", (Doubleday). I have also written extensively about him in
my books, "Most of All, They Taught Me Happiness" and "New
Genesis, Shaping a Global Spirituality".

Hopefully all the world's religions will join governments in the celebration of the fiftieth anniversary of the UN, and of the year 2000, our entry into the third millennium.

*

Hopefully, Pope John Paul II will visit the UN again in 1994, the International Year of the Family, or in 1995, the fiftieth anniversary of the UN, to give the world his vision of a spiritual third millennium. Prior to his visit he could hold another Assisi meeting to consult the heads of other religions.

*

The Pope is the only religious leader who can address officially the United Nations since he is a head of state, the Vatican state. He used this privilege only twice in forty-seven years.

*

In addition to the University for Peace there is a need for a University of Spirituality, Faith and Hope to illuminate the way of the world organization, enrich it and carry it successfully into the third millennium.

*

Every UN world conference should be preceded by a meeting of spiritual and indigenous people in order to remind governments and intellectuals of the spiritual and natural laws which should govern our lives on Earth. The sacred Ecology meeting which preceded UNCED II should serve as an example. The following is the Declaration it submitted to the summit meeting:

Declaration of the Sacred Earth Gathering
Rio - 92

The planet Earth is in peril as never before. With arrogance and presumption, humankind has disobeyed the laws of the Creator which manifest in the divine natural order.

The crisis is global. It transcends all national, religious, cultural, social, political and economic boundaries. The ecological crisis is a symptom of the spiritual crisis of the human being, arising from ignorance. The responsibility of each human being today is to choose between the force of darkness and the force of light. We must therefore transform our attitudes and values, and adopt a renewed respect for the superior law of Divine Nature.

Nature does not depend on human beings and their technology. It is human beings who depend on Nature for survival. Individuals and governments need to evolve "Earth Ethics" with a deeply spiritual orientation or the Earth will be cleansed.

We believe that the universe is sacred because all is one. We believe in the sanctity and the integrity of all life and life forms. We affirm the principles of peace and non-violence in governing human behavior towards one another and all life.

We view ecological disruption as violent intervention into the web of life. Genetic engineering threatens the very fabric of life. We urge governments, scientists and industry to refrain from rushing blindly into genetic manipulation.

We call upon all political leaders to keep a spiritual perspective when making decisions. All leaders must recognize the consequences of their actions for the coming generations.

We call upon our educators to motivate the people towards harmony with nature and peaceful coexistence with all living beings. Our youth and children must be prepared to assume their responsibilities as citizens of tomorrow's world.

We call upon our brothers and sisters around the world to recognize and curtail the impulses of greed, consumerism and disregard of natural laws. Our survival depends on developing the virtues of simple living and sufficiency, love and compassion with wisdom.

We stress the importance of respecting all spiritual and cultural traditions. We stand for preservation of the habitats and life style of indigenous people and urge restraint from disrupting their communion with nature.

The World Community must act speedily with vision and resolution to preserve the Earth, Nature and humanity from disaster. The time to act is now. Now or never.

*

After a lifetime of service with the UN, this is the New Genesis which I see emerge from the world organization:

THE NEW GENESIS

And God saw that all nations of the Earth, black and white,
poor and rich, from North and South, from East and West
and of all creeds were sending their emissaries to a tall
glass house on the shores of the River of the Rising Sun,
on the island of Manhattan, to study together, to think
together and to care together for the world and all its
people.

And God said: that is good.
And it was the first day of the New Age of the earth.

And God saw that soldiers of peace were separating the
combatants of quarrelling nations, that differences were
being resolved by negotiation and reason instead of arms,
and that the leaders of nations were seeing each other,
talking to each other and joining their hearts, minds, souls
and strength for the benefit of all humanity.

And God said: that is good.
And it was the second day of the Planet of Peace

And God saw that humans were loving the whole Creation, the
stars and the sun, the day and the night, the air and the
oceans, the earth and the waters, the fishes and the fowl,
the flowers and the herbs, and all their human brethren
and sisters.

And God said: that is good.
And it was the third day of the Happy Planet.

And God saw that humans were suppressing hunger, disease,
ignorance and suffering all over the globe, providing each
human person with a decent, conscious and happy life, and
reducing the greed, the power and the wealth of the few.

And God said: that is good.
And it was the fourth day of the Planet of Justice.

And God saw that humans were living in harmony with their
planet and in peace with one another, wisely managing
their resources, avoiding waste, curbing excesses,
replacing hatred with love, greed with contentment,
arrogance with humility, division with cooperation,
and mistrust with understanding.

And God said: that is good.
And it was the fifth day of the Golden Planet.

And God saw that nations were destroying their arms, bombs,
missiles, warships and warplanes, dismantling their bases
and disbanding their armies, keeping only policemen of
peace to protect the good from the bad and the normal
from the mad.

And God said: that is good.
And it was the sixth day of the Planet of Reason.

And God saw humans restore God and the human person as the
Alpha and Omega, reducing institutions, beliefs, politics,
governments and all human entities to mere servants of
God and of the people. And God saw them adopt as their
supreme law: 'You shall love the God of the universe with
all your heart, all your soul, all your mind and all your
strength. You shall love your beautiful, miraculous planet
and treat it with infinite care. You shall love your human
brothers and sisters as yourself. There are no greater
commandments than these.'

And God said: that is good.
And it was the seventh day of the Planet of God.

*

I hope that the second World Parliament of Religions in 1993 will agree on a set of commandments to be addressed to all people, governments, groups and institutions. The following is a draft they could consider:

THE TWENTY GLOBAL COMMANDMENTS

The Ten Commandments to all Humans

1. You shall love each other, your planet, your family, the God of the universe, and your own miraculous life with all your heart, all your soul, all your mind and all your strength.

2. You shall practice truth, kindness, and tolerance towards each other.

3. You shall never kill a human brother or sister, not even in the name of a nation.

4. You shall not produce, trade, wear, or use any arms or instruments of violence.

5. You shall never be violent, neither physically, verbally nor mentally.

6. You shall respect the lives, peace, happiness, and uniqueness of all your human brothers and sisters.

7. You shall cooperate with each other, help each other, inspire each other.

8. You shall contribute your peace, love, and happiness to the peace, love and happiness of the human family.

9. You shall live in harmony with yourself, with your family, with nature and your environment, with all humanity, and with the God of the universe.

10. You shall live a responsible life in accord with the supreme interests of our planet and of the human family.

The Ten Commandments to all Groups and Institutions

1. You shall practice truth, tolerance, and respect towards each other.

2. You shall live in unity and diversity, cooperate with each other, and shall not subvert each other.

3. You shall harmonize your actions and interests with the supreme interests of our planet and of the human family.

4. You shall not produce, trade, possess, or use any arms.

5. You shall not practice violence, neither physical, verbal nor mental, and shall resolve your differences peacefully.

6. You shall never require killing, violence, or unethical behavior from your members.

7. You shall respect the United Nations Charter and the unanimous rules, recommendations, and codes of conduct and ethics agreed to by humanity universally.

8. You shall adopt internal laws and rules of ethics in accord with the supreme interests of our planet and of humanity.

9. You shall protect the sacred rights of the human person, and obey the universal human rights injunctions of the United Nations.

10. You shall ensure the internal peace, love, and happiness of your members, and live in harmony with our planet, with all humanity and with the God of the universe.

*

For myself, here are my creed and commitments:

I. MY CREED

1. I believe in the absolute sacredness, uniqueness and prodigy of each human life;

2. I believe that humanity on this miraculous, wondrous, life-teeming planet has a tremendous cosmic destiny to fulfill and that a major transformation is about to take place in our evolution;

3. I believe that unprecedented life-fulfillment, consciousness, transcendence, happiness and union with God and the universe are the true objectives of life. I believe that cooperation, commitment to life, altruism, and love are the means to that fulfillment;

4. I believe that an unprecedented, all-encompassing new evolutionary agenda now faces humanity, namely;

   a. The harmony between humanity and our planet.

   b. The harmony and peace of the human family.

   c. Our harmony with time.

   d. Our harmony with the heavens.

   e. Our personal, individual harmony.

5. I believe that the main power, inspiration and wish for this transformation rests with each of the 5.5 billion individuals of this planet;

6. I believe that humanity must now transcend its magnificent material and scientific achievements into the moral, affective and spiritual fields. The next frontiers of humanity will be the heart and the soul of which an even lesser percentage than that of the brain is being used;

7. I believe in humanity's capacity for unparalleled thinking, perception, inspiration, elevation, planning, cooperation and love for

184

the achievement of a major transformation by the year 2000, and the advent of a peaceful, a happy and spiritual third millennium;

8. I believe that humanity should hold a worldwide Bimillennium Celebration of Life in the year 2000.

II. MY COMMITMENTS

I commit myself:

1. To thank God every day for the unbelievable gift of life;

2. To take good care of the miraculous cosmic unit I have been given, physically, mentally, morally and spiritually;

3. To be a peaceful, loving, kind, happy and healthy person all my life;

4. To irradiate my peace, my happiness and my belief in life;

5. To defend the first universal, cosmic law: 'Thou shall not kill, not even in the name of a nation or a faith;

6. To give thanks to God and society for the privilege of life by contributing to a better, more just, kinder, happier and peaceful world;

7. To devote every moment of my life, every thought, every action and every movement of my heart to the transformation of our planet into a true wonder in the universe;

8. To leave behind me children, friends, actions, thoughts and works which will continue to help humanity's further ascent and transformation towards universal, cosmic, divine fulfillment.

9. To spend my spiritual life after death in doing good for my beloved planet Earth.

*

You may ask:
"What can I do to contribute to the spirituality of the world?"
Simply this:

Decide to be a Spiritual Person

Render others spiritual
Irradiate your spirituality
Treat every moment of your life
    with divine respect
Love passionately your Godgiven,
    miraculous life
Be endlessly astonished at
    your brief, breathtaking
    conciousness of the universe
Thank God every moment
    for the tremendous gift of life
Lift your heart to the heavens always
Be a cosmic, divine being
    an integral conscious
    part of the universe
Contemplate with wonder
    the miraculous Creation
    all around you
Fill your body, mind, heart and soul
    with divine trepidation
Know that you are coming from somewhere
    and that you are going somewhere
    in the universal stream of time
Be always open to the entire universe
Know yourself and the heaven
    and the Earth
Act spiritually
Think spiritually
Love spiritually
Treat every person and living being
    with humaneness and divine respect
Pray, meditate, practice the art
    of spiritual living
And be convinced of eternal life
    and resurrection

*

The Three Supreme Commandments

You shall love the God of the universe with all your heart, all your soul, all your mind, and all your strength.

You shall love your beautiful, miraculous planet and treat it with infinite care.

You shall love your human brothers and sisters as yourself.

There are no greater commandments than these.

*   *
*

10

The UN and the Future

In response to the Secretary-General's appeal for the fortieth anniversary of the UN, Canada, the USSR and a number of other countries convened meetings of some of their best minds to review the UN at forty. I pray that on the occasion of the fiftieth anniversary in 1995, all countries of the world will follow this example.

*

What is my greatest wish for the UN?

That the world will increase immensely its support for it, so that all humanity can be ushered peacefully into the next millennium.

*

For centuries the religions have claimed the allegiance of the people, promising them paradise but in reality causing some of the bloodiest wars on this planet. Now nations are doing the same and again the people fall for it. Do we never learn anything from history? Dear people, it is high time that you proclaim your allegiance to the planet and to the human family. Politics and governments must become the servants of that higher allegiance.

*

We must teach children to love this planet and their human family more than any group claiming their allegiance.

*

The world needs a science of love, of peace, of happiness, of hope, of life, of positive thinking, feeling, action and spirit for our mysterious journey in the universe. The first rudiments of such sciences can be found in the United Nations and in its agencies and universities.

*

If the years that have passed since World War II have been so bad - and in my opinion they were not so bad - let us make the remaining years of this century considerably better. Let us settle as many problems and conflicts as possible, and think the world anew.

*

1994 has been proclaimed by the UN International Year of the Family. 1995, year of the fiftieth anniversary of the UN, should be proclaimed International Year of the Family of Nations.

*

The UN has done a good job in many fields of vital concern to the planet and to humanity. But it must accelerate the pace. For example, in the field of human rights, we must obtain the following new, global rights:

- To peace.

- To a disarmed planet.

- Not to kill and not to be killed, not even in the name of a nation.

- Adherence by governments to their international treaties and obligations.

- To a proper planning of the future by governments and world agencies.

- To non-violence among all groups.

- To truth.

- To global education.

- To objective information, advertising and marketing.

- Of future generations .

- To a well-preserved planet.

- To non-development, preservation and conservation.

- Not to pay taxes for armaments and the military.

- To be exempt from military service.

- To life of other species.

- Of the Earth and implementation of the UN Charter of Nature.

- To planetary citizenship and world democratic government.

- To proper relationships with our Creator.

- To proper relationships with the total stream of time.

*

The UN will be more permanent than any nation because it is a long-term organization in the mainstream of evolution. Its transformation will always be on an upward path, in response to the new needs of evolution.

*

What a world it will be when all nations will begin to really cooperate for the good of this planet, for the happiness of all peoples and to the satisfaction of God and the cosmos! A completely new page of human history will then begin.

*

Nations are likely to go down. Not the UN which would be transformed into something better or replaced by a new generation world organization.

*

The French Declaration of Human Rights was considered at the time to be "a cacophony and an assemblage of empty words", but it changed the course of history. It will be the same with the UN's Charter and Declarations.

*

The first UN Environment Conference in 1972 in Stockholm was criticized for being a "Birdwatchers Conference". Twenty years later the second conference in Rio de Janeiro was attended by more than one hundred heads of state and by thirty thousand people!

*

When the big powers will break down, the UN will be here to pick up the pieces, the same way as Christianity was around when the powerful Roman Empire collapsed.

*

The international framework of the world is obsolete and antiquated, while the world has undergone the most gigantic changes in human history. Is it not time to have a serious look at the framework and to devise a new, better one?

*

Today the administrations of many cities in the world are much bigger than the administrations of many countries of the past. And yet, they are considered a normal activity, without any particular glory or fanfare.

Some day the same will be true of nations: they will simply be provincial administrations without any particular glory or fanfare.

And some day the same will be true of the world: the UN or world government will simply be a democratic planetary administration without any glory or fanfare.

Then the real question will arise: what are life and this planet all about? We will then be on our right cosmic way.

*

The UN is here to stay. It might be pushed around but it will not be pushed aside. And even if it were to disappear, the UN would leave giant footprints on the sands of time.

*

From a Bulletin of the United Nations Association of Southern California (1984):

"Mr. Lichenstein who spoke of waiving goodbye to the UN as it would sail into the sunset, has resigned as deputy permanent representative of the US to the UN. Mr. Lichenstein, not the UN, leaves New York."

*

The UN must become the primary world agency to develop a world-wide strategy for the elimination of waste, unproductive and harmful products and activities. We now need a true world economy with the highest world productivity, and not the chaos of national economies with their incredible waste, duplication and colossal military expenditures no longer necessary and justifiable at this point of entry into the global age.

*

The world has stopped launching Mayflowers. Very few new audacious ideas have seen the light of day since the end of World War II. East/West follies were the only show on Earth. How could we ever fall so low? The need for new ideas, for great ideas, for bold ideas for the further ascent of humanity is pressing.

*

For the first time in history we have a Utopia in operation: the UN. So let us make it work and become a success.

*

If the Utopians from the past resuscitated and saw the UN, they would exclaim: but this is it! This is my utopia!

*

Most of humanity works at making this planet Utopia. And it will succeed.

*

I feel like shouting to my government: you can capture my body, you can capture my pocketbook, you can capture my time, but you cannot capture my heart and soul.

*

Society, the media, the   brevity of our life and our involvement in our time make us attach undue importance to the events and people notable during our life. But they are all so transient. Only relevant are the birth of ideas and actions which are part of a long-term evolution. That can be well observed in the United Nations, and on this rests my faith in its ultimate success.

*

As long as people will love their race, their nation, their language, their culture, their political system, their religion, their corporation more than their planet and human family, there will be no hope for peace and justice on this Earth. The future world order lies in the people's hearts.

*

We need Alexanders, Caesars and Napoleons of peace.

*

Who will use the sword will perish by the sword. Who will use peace will be blessed with peace.

*

A prayer for the United Nations, inspired by William Penn's prayer for Philadelphia:
"And you, United Nations, latest born of human dreams. What love, what care, what service, what travail, what suffering and war has there been to bring you forth and preserve you from such as would abuse and defile you. Oh may you be kept from the evil that would overwhelm you: that faithful to the God of mercies, in the life of righteousness, you may be preserved to the end."

*

We must have patience and perseverance. God's love will not abandon the United Nations.

*

To make the UN succeed is the most important challenge of our time.

*

"The United Nations needs a tremendous expansion. The world needs a new generation Charter."

Harold Stassen
US signatory of the UN Charter

*

I often remember this answer of General de Gaulle to a journalist who asked him what he thought of international organizations:

"Regarding these organizations, it will be one of two things: either they will serve no purpose or they will serve a purpose. If they serve no purpose, except to provide good jobs for some people, then it will be for the good of these people, provided they will serve no purpose. If, on the other hand, these institutions serve a purpose, then it will be the end of France."

And after a moment of reflection, looking at the distant horizon as he used to do, he added:

"Everything has an end. Why should not France have an end too? Perhaps my mission was a last effort towards the summits. Perhaps I have written the last page of France's grandeur." [33]

*

When I was introduced as the man who was in charge of the fortieth anniversary of the UN, to an American who claimed to be an expert on UN affairs, he commented:

"There is not likely to be any fiftieth anniversary of the UN."

I snapped back:

"Yes, most definitely there will be one; in Vienna, or in Geneva where the UN might be transferred to if necessary."

*

Every UN world conference reveals increasingly the interdependence of all things: between humans and the planet, between development and the environment, between the past and the future, between wealth and poverty, between nations, between professions,

---

[33]   J.R. Tournoux, *La Tragédie du Général*, (Librairie Plon, Paris 1967), pp. 253

between religions, etc. The end-result of this incipient and accelerating understanding of our inter-active world will be determining for our planet's and humanity's future.

*

I will never forget a wise and melancholic remark made by Premier Zhou En Lai during the visit of the UN Secretary-General to Beijing in 1972. "I am sitting here surrounded by my advisers trying to figure out what they might be scheming against us in Moscow and in Washington. In Moscow, they are trying to figure out what Beijing and Washington might be scheming against them. And they are probably doing the same in Washington. But perhaps in reality no one is scheming against anyone!" And he concluded that the role of the UN Secretary-General as an intermediary between heads of states was extremely important. As I listened to him, I closed my eyes and visualized the day when in his huge office there will be an audio-TV system linked instantaneously with all his partners in the administration of planet Earth.

Twenty years later, there still does not exist such a system between heads of states, although consultations between some of them were almost instantaneous during the Iraq-Kuwait war. How many decades will it still require to emerge from this stoneage non-system of working-relations between heads of states? Multinational business is infinitely better organized.

*

Our whole future lies in getting rid of one little letter: From United Nations to United Nation.

*

Humanity is the architect of its own future. The UN is the first school of global architecture.

*

The world cannot continue to live in the old way. We must improve not only our science and technology but also our consciousness, our responsibility, our habits and ways of behaving on Earth. The UN is the spearhead and mirror of these improvements. The world organization must be strengthened, loved, used and strengthened a hundred times more.

*

Oh God, help us solve and avoid the man-made catastrophes of this planet, so that we can concentrate on its natural disasters.

*

At the entrance of the UN, one could affix the motto of the City of Paris:

"Fluctuat nec mergitur"
"It floats, and never sinks."

*

I once asked the organizers of the US Bicentennial Celebrations when they started to plan for the Bicentennial. They answered: "Right after World War II".

When will the world begin to prepare its Bimillennium Celebration?

*

- **50 years** of life for an insect would be an eternity.

- **50 years** is more than half of an average human life.

- **50 years** in the life of many nations and of the United Nations is all they had so far.

- **50 years** is one hundredth of the civilized history of humanity.

- **50 years** is a mere minute of the 3 million years of human evolution.

- **50 years** is no more than a second in the past 4.5 billion years of this planet and of the 5 billion years still to come.

- **50 years** is a mere speck of time in the 10 to 15 billion years since the beginning of the universe.

Why give up hope, therefore?

*

In ten to twenty years from now there will be no longer any wars between nations on this planet. However there will remain violence in individuals, in families, in cities, in nations, in nature and the global spaces of our planet.[34] The UN must therefore be reconverted into the non-violent, holistic peace organization of this planet.

*

"I have no concern that the United Nations will disappear. The UN is here to stay. This is one victory we have won, one great progress over the League of Nations."

Secretary-General *Javier Perez de Cuellar*

*

Irrealistic, idealistic fools are not those who request the total destruction of armaments on this planet, but those who believe that nations will agree on arms control or limitation. If both categories should be irrealistic, I prefer to belong to the first one.

*

We should not speak of arms race, but of arms addiction.

We should not speak of arms control, but of arms destruction.

We should not speak of war control, but of war suppression.

We should not speak of peace-keeping forces but of the demilitarization of this planet.

*

The problems of this world will become so colossal that the big powers will have to cooperate. Then the UN will become at long last effective, the world peaceful and disarmament possible.

*

When I think of all the gigantic global problems which face this planet, the information, knowledge, experience and actions which are needed to cope with them, I consider it simply insane that some people think that the world would be better off without the United

---

[34]   In July 1992, during the UNCED Conference in Rio Sushil Kumar, spiritual leader of the Jains, and I co-founded a World Movement of Non-Violence for Peace and the Environment.

Nations and its specialized agencies. A statesman worthy of this name should recommend on the contrary an unprecedented. novel, resounding, path-breaking Marshall type quantum jump of the United Nations. Attacks against the UN, placing it on the defensive, are one of the greatest blemishes of our time. Governments should be ashamed and the people scared at a retreat from international cooperation. It could lead to World War III. We need infinitely more international cooperation, not less. We must not repeat the mistake toward the League of Nations.

*

Today news, messages, books, films, ideas, poems, as well as an exemplary life can reach the whole world. How sad however, that what reaches the world through the media is predominantly:

- bad news;

- negative, pessimistic information;

- sensational, prefabricated "best-sellers";

- horror, violence and war films;

- negative, hostile ideas;

- seldom any poems;

- seldom an exemplary life;

This applies to the coverage of the United Nations too. The human will for life must be iron-strong to withstand such beatings. It is a true miracle that the human society has not yet crumbled at the hands of the media. But how long will it resist?

It is most urgent that the best minds of this planet tackle this problem which stands monumentally in the way of a better world.

*

Abolition of slavery was considered impossible hundreds of years ago.

Equality between men and women was considered impossible a hundred years ago.

Reconciliation between France and Germany was considered impossible fifty years ago.

Reconciliation between the US and the USSR was considered impossible ten years ago.

Yet it all became true.

Today friendship between the Arabs and Jews is considered impossible.

Today the demilitarization of the entire planet is considered impossible

Today total peace is considered impossible

Today world democratic government is considered impossible

And yet it will all become true.

*

Seen from the United Nations, the world is in even worse shape than the media and the people generally think. But there is also a lot of hope and a growing number of people who share the UN's ideals. That is the world's brightest aspect.

*

The sun to humans:

"Look at my nine planets. Three of them are pure ice. Two are masses of gas. Two are fiery balls and one is icy rock. On only one, namely yours, the Earth, after sending out my rays for billions of years have I succeeded to produce life, a very rare phenomenon in the universe. And see what a mess you have done with it! I am ashamed of you. You are playing with my Creation without the slightest comprehension of the miracle it is and of the magnitude of your misdoings. If you continue you will lose the right to call yourself the proud human race. You will be doomed as a cosmic failure, as a misfit, as an evolutionary aberration.

*

Since 1945 the world has produced only three great ideas: the United Nations, the Marshall Plan and the European Community.

Capitalism and Communism have occupied so overwhelmingly the forefront of the world that no one has dared to come up with any other bold new idea. Please young people, awake and break the imprisonment in which you are held. We need a new youth movement before the end of this millennium.

*

During the US Bicentennial I was shown a record of the debates which lasted ten years until the adoption of the US Constitution. They were so far apart, so shocking, so violent and full of hatred that the debates in the UN today look angelic in comparison! It gave me hope for the future.

*

There can be no downward alternatives to the UN, only upward ones.

*

Humanity progresses mainly through paradigmic individuals and institutions. Maximum inspiration is given when paradigmic individuals are at the helm of paradigmic institutions. John XXIII, John Paul II, Dag Hammarsjköld and U Thant are examples of such fortunate occurrences.

*

The League of Nations was right, not Hitler, Mussolini, nor the Japanese war lords who destroyed it.

The United Nations is right, not those who wish to diminish or destroy it.

Even if the UN, like the League of Nations, were to go under, God forbid, it would still be right and would be reborn in a new, better form, according to the laws of evolution. No one can go for long against evolution and human ascent.

*

As a first step in disarmament, at least a ceiling on military expenditures should be decreed world-wide. No nation should be allowed to spend more than one percent of its gross national product on armaments and the military. Japan already does it. It is one of the main causes of its prosperity and rise as a world economic power.

*

In Constitution Hall in Philadelphia, one sees the President's chair which has a half-sun with golden rays painted on its back. Benjamin Franklin was very old when the constitution was finally adopted. He addressed the Assembly in these terms:

"I have often, in the course of the session and the vicissitudes of my hopes and fears as to its issue, looked at the back of the President's chair without being able to tell whether the sun painted on it was rising or setting. But now at length I have the happiness to know that it is a rising sun."

I hope that a replica of that chair will be offered by the City of Philadelphia to the United Nations for use by the President of the United Nations Constitutional Assembly for the world.

*

Where is the great statesperson, a George Washington, who will proclaim:

"Enough is enough! We cannot go on like this. We must convene a world constitutional assembly."

I believe he or she will arise soon.

*

Most world ventures, new institutions and novel ideas I was associated with during my life, had very difficult beginnings. They were usually opposed by nations, but with time and perseverance, most of them succeeded and were recognized as essential instruments of human progress. On the average it takes from ten to twenty years for a new global problem to be recognized and equipped with a decent world institutional arrangement. The supra-national University for Peace is one of the latest ventures. For ten years, few were those who believed in it. Today it has reached the take-off stage. In a few years if will be one of the most extraordinary universities on Earth.

Let us hope that henceforth new global problems will take fewer years to be recognized.

*

One of my dreams is to see the University for Peace in Costa Rica become the first modern school for heads of states where they would be taught to manage our planet in peace, justice and efficiency. The only other school for heads of states that ever existed on this planet was created by Confucius in ancient China.

*

The future evolvement of the UN system must respond to these planet-wide, evolutionary needs:

1. Perception: world data, information from the infinitely large to the infinitely small;

2. Recognition and determination of trends, patterns, networks and systems;

3. Visions, objectives, future images of the total world system, of human and planetary evolution;

4. The motor system: decisions, resolutions, volition, inspiration;

5. Identification of the means to act, from large institutions to the individual, from huge common resources to single voluntary actions;

6. Concrete action, from global to local, from the total to the individual;

7. Evaluation of action and progress;

8. Constant course correction.

*

Since the fortieth anniversary of the UN, at least 16 good things have happened:

1. The end of the cold war.

2. The reunification of Germany.

3. Several summit meetings between the Presidents of the US and the USSR (Russia).

4. A first reduction and destruction of atomic arms.

5. A wave of peace settlements in Afghanistan, Cambodia, Nicaragua, Western Sahara and El Salvador.

6. A revival of the effectiveness of the Security Council in response to the unilateral invasion of Kuwait by Iraq.

7. The independence of Namibia.

8. The end of apartheid.

9. The use of important UN peacekeeping forces in the internal conflicts of a member country, Yugoslavia.

10. The creation of a Central American Parliament and regular meetings between the Presidents of the Central American Republics.

11. The announcement by the President of the U.S. of work towards the creation of a free trade area from Alaska to Tierra del Fuego.

12. The declaration of the 1990's as the decade of International Law and of Cultural Development.

13. A third disarmament Decade is launched in the new political landscape resulting from the end of the cold war.

14. A new Development Strategy is adopted for the 1990's.

15. The Security Council held its first meeting ever at the heads of states level. It requested the Secretary-General to prepare his analysis and recommendations on ways of strengthening the capacity of the UN for preventive diplomacy, for peacemaking and peace-keeping by July, 1992.

16. France suspended its atomic tests.

*

There are several more good things and dates to come:

1992:   - The second UN world conference on the environment and development at the summit level in Brazil;

         - The five hundredth anniversary of the discovery of America;

         - The International Year of Space; together with the conference on the environment, this will make 1992 the first cosmic year in human history, namely an attempt at a total, comprehensive appraisal of our place in the universe and of our planetary habitat;

1993:   - The abolition of borders in Western Europe and the entry into force of the political European Community;

- The second World Parliament of Religions, 100 years after the first one in Chicago in 1983;

- The International Year of the World's Indigenous People;

- The second World Conference on Human rights in Vienna;

1994:   - The International Year of the Family;

1995:   - The historical fiftieth anniversary of the UN, a unique occasion for a fundamental rethinking and strengthening of the UN on the eve of the Bimillennium. It should be proclaimed Year of the Family of Nations;

- The fourth World Conference on Women;

1996:   - The return of Hong Kong to China. This year should be proclaimed International year or Prevention. The world is too much geared at healing, repairing and resolving rather than preventing sicknesses, accidents, disasters, conflicts and environmental deterioration. World policies and peoples' attitudes must be shifted to prevention;

1997:   - This year is still free. I would recommend a second World Youth Conference be held, twelve years after the first one in 1985, to allow the youth of today to express its wishes, visions, ideas and ideals for the 21st century and the third millennium which will be theirs;

1998:   - The fiftieth anniversary of the Universal Declaration of Human Rights;

1999:   - The hundredth anniversary of the first World Peace Congress in The Hague;

- The entry into force of the new Panama Canal Treaty;

2000:   - The celebration of the Bimillennium and our entry into the third millennium;

At long last, we seem to be on the right path. Let us accelerate the momentum with a host of more settlements and preparations, in order to enter the third millennium with a clean slate and with great new visions, ideas and actions for a millennium of peace, justice, well-being and human fulfillment on our miraculous, perhaps unique, lovely planet in the universe.

I urgently recommend the creation of the following new UN agencies:[35]

World Disarmament Agency

World Agency for the Handicapped

World Agency for the Elderly

World Women's Agency

World Youth Agency

World Energy Agency (incorporating the IAEA)

World Transportation Agency

World Ocean and Seabed Agency (still not ratified)

World Consumer Agency

World Migration and Refugee Agency
 (incorporating the UNHCR)

World Global Data Agency

World Outer Space Agency

World Financial Facility for the Environment

World Climate Organization   (incorporating the WMO)
*

[35]   More ideas for the future of the UN can be found in chapter 13 of my book, *"The Birth of a Global Civilization"*, and the **Peace Plan 1992 - 2010**, in my novel, *"First Lady of the World"*

So much more can be done by a considerably strengthened United Nations and its agencies. I am thinking for example of the University for Peace in demilitarized Costa Rica, one of the most beautiful creations of the UN. It was proposed by the President of Costa Rica in the fall of 1979 and entered into existence in April of 1981. Yet eleven years later, only 32 out of 179 governments have ratified it and only a handful have given it any finance. The first University for Peace on this planet is the smallest and poorest university in existence, while thousands of military academies are thriving. It almost seems that governments are afraid of peace. Yet the time has come when the world needs the same science of peace, strategy of peace and methodology for peace which were developed by Napoleon and Clausewitz for war and which are taught in military academies. Thirty years later the first curriculum I proposed for the University for Peace amounts only to two Masters Programs in International Relations and in Ecology for Peace taught to a total of sixty students. I tell the students that Jesus did wonders with only twelve apostles and that each of them should at least become a head of state. Governments should be ashamed for their scandalous lack of support of the first University for Peace on this planet.

*

On the occasion of the fiftieth anniversary of the UN, a compendium of all unresolved conflicts, disputes, problems, unratified treaties and agreements should be drawn up by the UN Secretariat to serve as a priority agenda for the remaining years of this millennium.

*

There is nothing more fascinating on Earth than to see the birth of a central administration for this planet and for humanity by global servants from more than 175 nations! All the great dreamers, saints and philosophers of the past would be astonished and elated by it. And yet, nowhere in our blind contemporary society is there a single school or training place for this new, crucial administration. The University for Peace remains so far largely unimplemented due to the indifference of most nations, while it should occupy a priority place on the actions of the community of nations.

*

The future world order rests in the hands of a new generation of young people well educated about the globe and its inhabitants and trained and inspired to love and to care passionately for the globe and for humanity. This is what the mushrooming global education all around the world and the University for Peace are on the way of doing.

*

Through disarmament and demilitarization we must reduce the number of countries able to wage war, and increase the number of those eager to construct peace.

*

A remark by a student of the University for Peace:
"I strongly believe that a nuclear-weapon free and non-violent world cannot be built by those who build arms."
He is absolutely right. This is why the UN should concentrate not so much on the destruction of existing arms but rather attack arms production, i.e. take the problem right at its source.

*

Multinational corporate business is nothing compared with the mind-boggling multinational business of the UN system. To make profit is rather easy. To build a moral, just and well-ordered happy society is quite another challenge. Unfortunately, multinational corporate business is often in contradiction with the objectives of the United Nations, instead of being supportive and cooperative. Sooner or later they will have to come around, forced by the new planetary imperatives from which there is no escape. Given the impacts of multinational corporate business on world conditions, a world conference should be urgently held on Multinational Business,Peace, Justice, Progress and the Environment.

*

If George Washington were alive today and saw the world chaos in which we live on the eve of the third millennium, he would probably use the same words he had in a letter to John Jay when he feared that:

"...the monster, sovereignty, would put to rout the efforts of the US constitutional convention..."

We would not be even able to show him today a world constitutional convention in session. Where are the Benjamin Franklins, Thomas Jeffersons, John Jays and George Washingtons today? They would expect to see a substantial progress of world political order since their time. Instead they would see a lot of regress. The political leaders and thinkers of today should be ashamed.

*

In the world of today there are two political systems superior, I would say far superior to the United Nations: The European Community and the federal system. They should both be considered for urgent introduction, if the UN remains stifled, grossly unimplemented, denied any institutional growth and legislative, executive and judicial powers, isolated from public representation, and at the mercy of national financing. No child would survive with such unconcerned, stingy parents as are today's nations. This joke has lasted long enough and must come to an end. A new world political system must be considered, capable to cope with the colossal problems in the coming third millennium, of which the world is pregnant with today.

*

If the United Nations is not rapidly strengthened and given substantially increased powers and secure financial resources, I would urge the world to consider the European Community with its agreed limitations of national sovereignty and huge independent resources as a foundation of the future world community and planetary order. Non-European countries would be admitted progressively until the Community would encompass the entire world. This policy should be announced at the latest by the year 2000 and the adjective "European" should be dropped from its name to become simply the Community. Jean Monnet announced this course at the end of his Memoirs:

> "Have I said clearly enough that the Community we
> created is not an end in itself? It is a process of change,
> continuing in that same process which in an earlier period
> produced our national forms of life. The sovereign nations
> of the past cannot ensure their own progress or control their

own future. And the Community itself is only a stage on the way of the organized world of tomorrow."[36]

*

Humans are the most advanced perceptory cosmic units of the universe. Through humans, the cosmos tries to do something very special on our wonderful, unique planet. If we understand that, we will succeed. If we don't, we will fail and the cosmos will try something else. It is as simple as that. The choice is ours.

*   *

*

---

[36]   See chapter thirteen of my book, *"The Birth of a Global Civilization"*, (1991, World Happiness and Cooperation)

Epilogue

My Last Days at the UN

Costa Rica - 3 March, 1986

Today I prayed and thanked God for His blessings at the early morning mass in the Cathedral of San José.

At midday I walked in the heavenly, tropical woods of the University for Peace on its inspiring hills, thanking God for one more, great, miraculous gift:

I received the offer today to become the Chancellor of the University for Peace, three days before my retirement from the UN!

Oh God, I have the impression that You are caring a lot for me, saving me from death during World War II and making me an instrument of Your peace until my death and perhaps even beyond.

*

4 March 1986
San José, Costa Rica, and New York

United Nations Press release

The International Council of the University of Peace appointed today Rodrigo Carazo as Council President for a period of two years. Mr. Carazo is a former President of Costa Rica.

The Council, the governing body of the University, also appointed Robert Muller as University Chancellor. Mr. Muller has been Assistant Secretary-General for the commemoration of the fortieth anniversary of the United Nations.

The University of Peace was established in 1980 by the General Assembly in resolution 35/55.

Under terms of its Charter, the University's aim is to promote "the spirit of understanding, tolerance and peaceful coexistence, to stimulate co-operation among peoples and help lessen obstacles and threats to world peace and progress".

To that end, it "shall contribute to the great universal task of educating for peace by engaging in teaching, research, post-graduate training and dissemination of knowledge fundamental to the full development of the human person and societies through the interdisciplinary study of all matters relating to peace".

The proposal to establish the institution was made by Mr. Carazo, as President of Costa Rica, in an address to the General Assembly in 1978.

The University is authorized to grant master's degrees and doctorates under terms established by the Council.

*

Costa Rica, 5 March 1986

Today, I met at the University for Peace two students who had received the first world academic diplomas: the University for Peace's Master degree in peace communications. It was a very moving event. The University Council put this question to the students: "What difference did this education make to you? Has any change occurred in you as journalists?"

One student answered:

"Yes, I was used to report mostly bad news as I was taught to. Now I write stories about good things, trying to educate other people about the good things I have learned."

"Could you give an example?"

"Yes, I have just written a story how peasant women in Costa Rica organize themselves to get better prices for their agricultural products instead of being exploited by middlemen. With that story, I can help poor women in my own country, Colombia, do the same."

The second student gave similar examples of her transformation from negative to positive news reporting.

Both spoke with enthusiasm of the World Peace News Service and of the International Radio for Peace created at the University.

*

New York, 11 March 1986

On my 63rd birthday I feel 30 years younger because I embark upon the new exciting adventure as Chancellor of the University for Peace in Costa Rica, an unpaid job, an almost impossible job, since the University has only meager financial resources.

But I like impossible jobs. Perhaps this is what I was born for and why I am still alive.

May I count on my many readers and friends to help me succeed. My appointment is theirs too. It is our common success as lovers and defenders of the peace of this beautiful planet and of humanity.

*

I received this birthday card from my secretary:

11 March 1986

"To dear Mr. Muller, who has effectively taught the lesson through his writings that "life is what we make it" - and you have made yours full of purpose and meaning - my very best wishes for great undertakings in the freedom of retirement..."

Grace Balmaceda

*

Letter from the head of one of the UN Specialized agencies:

New York, 20 March 1986

"Dear Robert,
I learned that you were going to retire.
Let me use this occasion to send you my best wishes for the new phase of your life which is about to begin. You can look back with pride and satisfaction on the 38-year phase that you are closing. No one has served better than you the cause of global understanding in the framework of the United Nations. Your merits are immense and you will, through your excellent books, continue to influence contemporary thinking about international cooperation."

Arpad Bogsch - Director General
World Intellectual Property Organization

*

Easter, 30 March 1986

My last Easter as a UN official. Tomorrow will be my last day. I am glad that I complete my world service on a day of resurrection and hope.

I am thinking of Teilhard de Chardin who died on an Easter Sunday, day of resurrection, according to his wishes. And of Father de Breuvery, his companion, who told me on the eve of his own death that he wanted a mass in white, a mass of joy and resurrection for his funeral.

May I also express the wish that my last service will be a mass of joy and resurrection.

My Easter prayer:

I pray that there will be no one left on this Earth who hates the UN.

I pray that the American people will awaken and instill a new spirit in the great universal organization which they helped create.

I pray God to bless the United Nations, as Pope John Paul II did with tears in his eyes when he left the UN after his historical visit.

I pray that all the schools of planet Earth will teach the children about the UN.

I pray that all human beings on this planet will help fulfill the dreams of peace, justice and prosperity of their world organization.

I pray that all humans will contribute their peace, love, happiness and kindness to a better world.

I pray that all nations on Earth will prepare a beautiful world-wide golden jubilee of the UN in 1995 and a Bimillennium Celebration of Life and Peace in the year 2000.

*

United Nations, 31 March 1986

Heart overflowing with love
Head filled with thoughts
And God overhead
I am walking the last time
After thousands of times
To my beloved United Nations
The star of human loves and dreams.

In the tall House of Mica on the River of the Rising Sun where all the nations of Mother Earth meet, I sing to humanity and its future peace and justice, I sing to the miracle of life, I sing to the beauty of the Earth. Oh may God and the people hear my songs!

I thank you Oh God for having retired me to put good order in my affairs, to fulfill my remaining tasks with great courage and great zeal, thinking not of what passes but of what remains.

I say this with tears in my eyes:

"Dear friends, please continue my life-work, support
and help the United Nations and make it the guiding star
of this beautiful planet, and of its proud human race."

To those who think that I worked a lot and who appreciated my work, please thank me by supporting the United Nations and its University for Peace. This is all I beg from you.

Even if I have not succeeded during my life-time, at least it will have paved the way for those who will follow. My dearest wish is to be an example to them, my greatest hope is that they will succeed.

I will continue to pester the world with ideas and proposals until its leaders will change course for the good of all peoples and of the Earth.

If you love me, please love the UN and raise it to the sky.

*

I placed today the first draft of this Testament on the altar of the UN Meditation Room, asking God to bless it.

> The Lord gave me the UN
> The Lord has taken away from me the UN
> Blessed be the Lord
> Thy will be done.

*

Six Years Later

Rio de Janeiro, 29 May 1992

I was invited to the second UN Conference on Environment and Development in Rio de Janeiro to see how the baby Environment had grown since the UN gave it birth more than two decades ago, and also to deliver new phrophecies.

When I met there the spiritual leader of the 20 million Jains in India, Sushil Kumar, I asked him:

"Does there exist a world movement for non-violence?"

He answered, no

" Why don't you create one?"

He looked at me astonished and said:

"This is the great idea I have been waiting for. I shall do it. Would you accept to be its co-founder? Thus East and West will meet."

I accepted, wherupon he told me this:

"Yesterday I visited the huge 100 foot high Christ erected on a hill overlooking Rio. As I stood before him, I closed my eyes, lifted my arms and asked him: 'Dear God, tell me what else I can do?' And I heard this answer: Tomorrow someone will come who will tell you. And here you are telling me."

*

Rio de Janeiro, 5 June 1992

When in turn I visited Christ's statue, I did the same, closed my eyes, lifted my arms and knew that the answer to my prayer would be given.

The following morning I was asked to speak at the Global Forum to a new movement which had just been created to endow humanity with a Global Heart. A dream I had harbored for many years was fulfilled and Christ's message to me was to help it succeed.

*

Costa Rica, 10 June 1992

I received today a cable inviting me to participate in a meeting at the UN in New York on 30 June to prepare the fiftieth, golden, anniversary of the UN!

Thank you, Oh World, for still using me as your servant. Thank you, Oh God, for fulfilling yet another dream.

*

THE END ?
(of course not)

MY DREAM 2000

I dream
>That on 1 January 2000
>The whole world will stand still
>In prayer, awe and gratitude
>For our beautiful, heavenly Earth
>And for the miracle of human life.

I dream
>That young and old, rich and poor,
>Black and white
>Peoples from North and South
>From East and West
>From all beliefs and cultures
>Will join their hands, minds and hearts
>In an unprecedented, universal
>Bimillennium Celebration of Life.

I dream
>That the year 2000
>Will be declared World Year of Thanksgiving
>>by the United Nations.

I dream
>That during the year 2000
>Innumerable celebrations and events
>Will take place all over the globe
>To gauge the long road covered by humanity
>To study our mistakes
>And to plan the feats
>Still to be accomplished
>For the full flowering of the human race
>In peace, justice and happiness.

I dream
>That the few remaining years
>To the Bimillennium
>Be devoted by all humans, nations and
>>institutions
>To unparalleled thinking, action,
>Inspiration, elevation,
>Determination and love
>To solve our remaining problems
>And to achieve
>A peaceful, united human family on Earth.

I dream
>That the third millennium
>Will be declared
>And made
>Humanity's First Millennium of Peace.

*

I recommend that in 1995 the Preparatory committee for the fiftieth anniversary of the UN, which consists of all members of the UN, be converted into the Preparatory Committee for the Celebration of the year 2000.

*   *
*

APPENDIX 1

Highlights of the United Nations[37]

The United Nations was created to prevent war by providing Governments with means for regular contact, cooperation, and collective action. Though international conflicts have continued, over the last decades Governments have been able to agree on common positions in a surprising number of matters. In the process, the essential foundations for a peaceful world have been strengthened. The United Nations system has become the world's main source of international law, codifying and creating more of it in four decades than in all previous history. In the area of human rights, its work has been pioneering. The protection of human rights is acknowledged now to be a legitimate concern of the international community: global standards have been set and binding agreements negotiated for the observance of a wide range of basic rights.

The United Nations has eased the passage to freedom of millions of people in former colonial territories, and focused international attention and support for ancient societies transforming themselves with modern science and technology. It has led a worldwide cooperative effort to deal with such urgent problems as population growth and environmental hazards, the effects of which transcend all national borders. For millions caught unprotected in the tumultuous processes of change - poor children, political refugees, victims of disaster - the organization has brought the healing touch of attention and care. The chronology below is by no means a comprehensive listing; it merely indicates the vast scope of United Nations activities over the last decades.

---

[37]   Update of a document published on the occasion of the fortieth anniversary of the UN.

1945: On June 26 the Charter of the United Nations is signed in San Francisco. The Second World War has ended in Europe but continues in Asia; its end there coincides with the terrible dawn of the nuclear age. The UN, created on October 24 is at the center of a system of specialized agencies, some newly founded, others created decades earlier.

1946: In January, the *General Assembly* meets for the first time, in London, and elects the members of the *Security Council*, the *Economic and Social Council*, and the *International Court of Justice*. The first resolution the Assembly adopts is on disarmament, on the peaceful use of nuclear energy. Over the next four decades, as the arms race spirals upward, the organization keeps the problem high on the international agenda. Other major problems considered by the first Assembly: decolonization, racial discrimination in South Africa, and the growing violence between Arabs and Jews in Palestine. In October the Assembly meets in New York, picked as headquarters for the organization. It establishes the *United Nations Children's Fund*. The *Trusteeship Council* is set up.

1947: The Assembly adopts a plan that would, at the end of the British Mandate in Palestine in 1948, partition it into an Arab State and a Jewish State with Jerusalem under UN administration. The organization's involvement in the region continues unabated over the next decades as it seeks peace with equity for all parties involved.

1948: The *Universal Declaration of Human Rights* is adopted without opposition in the Assembly, marking the first time in history that such a document is endorsed by the international community. The cold war is at its height and the Secretary-General reports that the UN is virtually the only place where East and West have regular contact. UN military observers are sent to the Middle East and south Asia. International statistical services are resumed after an interruption of almost a decade as the UN Secretariat begins to collect, analyze, and publish data from around the world about the world and human condition.

1949: Consultations initiated at the UN lead to a resolution of the crisis over Western access to the divided city of Berlin. The Assembly creates an agency to look after the welfare of the hundreds of thousands of Palestinian refugees in the Middle East. The UN and the specialized agencies begin the *Expanded Program of Technical Assistance* to help economic and social development in poorer countries. Experts from more that 50 countries attend the *UN Scientific Conference on Conservation and Utilization of Resources*.

1950: The Security Council calls on member states to help the southern part of Korea repel invasion from the north, (The Soviet Union is absent from the Council then, in protest against the exclusion of the People's Republic of China from the UN). At the initiative of the UN, the *World Census Program* gets under way, aiming at a global head-count every decade: the first such assessment in history. The *UN Cartographic Office* is set up and coordinates with governments involved in producing a map of the world on the millionth scale. The Economic and Social Council (ECOSOC) adopts the *Standard International Trade Classification*, the basis on which all statistics on world trade are now gathered.

1951: The Office of *UN High Commissioner for Refugees* established by the General Assembly, takes over from the *International Refugee Organization*. The conference convened by the Assembly adopts the *Convention on Refugees*, spelling out their rights and international standards for their treatment. The ECOSOC Regional Commission for Asia initiates studies of the Mekong River that lead to one of the largest river basin development projects attempted internationally.

1952: The General Assembly broadens its consideration of racial discrimination in South Africa to take up the entire question of apartheid, overriding South African objections that it is a matter entirely within its domestic jurisdiction. Over the next four decades, the organization will be at the forefront of international efforts to fight a system of racism that the Assembly terms a "crime against humanity." The UN produces the first in a series of reports on the *World Social Situation*.

1953: Armistice in Korea results from initiatives made at the UN. The *UN Opium Conference* in New York adopts an international protocol to control the production, trade, and use of the drug.

1954: The Secretary-General initiates quiet, and ultimately successful, negotiations for the release of American airmen held as prisoners of war in China. The *World Population Conference* convened by ECOSOC brings over 450 experts to Rome. They adopt no resolutions, but it is evident that current knowledge of population trends is insufficient for decisions on economic and social policy. First signs of a thaw in the cold war appear as the ECOSOC Regional Commission for Europe takes up trade relations between different economic systems   The UN High Commissioner for Refugees wins the first of two Nobel Peace Prizes; the second is awarded in 1981.

1955: The first *UN Congress on Prevention of Crime and Treatment of Offenders* sets minimum standards for the treatment of prisoners and for the training of personnel for correctional institutions. The first international conference on the *Peaceful Uses of Atomic Energy* convenes in Geneva and initiates a broad range of cooperation in the field.

1956: War in the Middle East over the Suez Canal is ended with the deployment of a UN peacekeeping force in the Sinai. A UN-supervised plebiscite in British Togoland leads to the merging of that Territory with the Gold Coast to form the new State of Ghana.

1957: In the wake of Sputnik, the General Assembly takes up the peaceful uses of outer space. In the following years, it elaborates a new body of law to cover the exploration and use of outer space, including the Moon and other celestial bodies. *The International Atomic Energy Agency*, created by the General Assembly, begins work with headquarters in Vienna.

1958: The *UN Observer Group* helps defuse a Lebanon crisis. The *Inter-Governmental Maritime Consultative Organization* begins work as a UN specialized agency, setting safe standards for shipping. The first *UN Conference on the Law of the Sea* adopts four landmark Conventions. French Togoland becomes independent after a UN-supervised plebiscite.

1959: The General Assembly adopts the *Declaration of the Rights of the Child*. A Special Fund established by the General Assembly works in tandem with the *Expanded Program of Technical Assistance* to help developing countries explore areas into which private and public capital can be attracted. A UN-supervised plebiscite in the British Cameroons results in a part of the Territory's being incorporated into Nigeria and another into the Cameroons.

1960: With the entry into the UN of 17 newly independent Territories, 16 of them African, the General Assembly assumes a much more active role in the process of decolonization. It adopts the *Declaration on the Granting of Independence to Colonial Countries and Peoples,* saying colonialism is a denial of basic human rights and calling for its swift end. At the request of the newly independent State of Congo, the largest ever UN peacekeeping force takes the field in an effort to save that mineral rich country from destabilization and preserve its territorial integrity.

1961: Acknowledging that economic and social development in the poorer countries is basic to the achievement of international peace and security, the General Assembly declares the 1960's the *UN Development Decade.* UN capacity to deal with development problems is vastly increased during the decade.

1962: The Secretary-General plays a key role in resolving U.S.-Soviet confrontation over the issue of nuclear missiles in Cuba. The UN takes over administration of Dutch West New Guinea before transferring power to Indonesia. The *UN Observer Mission* aids peace efforts in Yemen.

1963: The UN and the Food and Agriculture Organization (FAO) set up the *World Food Program* to provide food and other commodity aid to needy countries, drawing on surpluses in donor countries. The Security Council calls for voluntary arms embargo against South Africa.

1964: *UN Conference on Trade and Development* declares trade a "primary instrument of development," and calls for a permanent secretariat to focus on the web of problems involved. A UN peacekeeping force is sent to Cyprus to keep communal peace. It stays over the following years as talks under UN auspices seek a peaceful solution.

1965: The *UN Observer Mission* helps disengagement of forces after war between India and Pakistan. Technical assistance activities get a big boost with the merger of the *Expanded Program* (1949) and the *Special Fund* (1959) into the *UN Development Program* as the major channel of funding for the specialized agencies in the UN system. UNDP assumes an important coordinating role and extends a network of "resident representatives" to help aid delivery around the world. **UNICEF is awarded the Nobel Peace Prize.**

1966: Two major covenants on human rights are adopted, one covering Civil and Political Rights and the other Economic, Social and Cultural Rights. The former has an "Optional Protocol" allowing individual complaints to be considered by the International Human Rights Committee. Together, the two binding instruments cover most of the rights included in the 1948 Universal Declaration of Human Rights. The Security Council for the first time in UN history, imposes mandatory sanctions against Southern Rhodesia, where a racist white minority government unilaterally declared independence from Britain in 1965. The Assembly ends South Africa's mandate over the Territory of South West Africa, saying it has failed to fulfill its obligations.

1967: After war erupts again in the Middle East, the Security Council adopts Resolution 242, which calls for withdrawal of forces from occupied territories and recognizes the right of all States in the area to security. It becomes a widely accepted basis for a settlement of the Middle East problem. The General Assembly, meeting in special session, sets up a UN council to administer South West Africa.

1968: On the 20th anniversary of the Universal Declaration, the *International Conference on Human Rights* is convened by the General Assembly in Teheran. The first worldwide governmental meeting on the whole range of human rights, it reaffirms the Declaration, and chalks out further priorities for UN action.

1969: The *Convention on Elimination of All Forms of Racial Discrimination*, adopted by the General Assembly in 1965, comes into force. Parties to the Convention condemn racial discrimination and apartheid and undertake to adopt policies for their elimination without delay.

1970: The *International Development Strategy* is adopted for the Second Development Decade declared by the General Assembly. Targets are set for different groups of countries and for increases in aid and industrial and agricultural production. The General Assembly adopts the first internationally agreed set of principles on the vast area of seabed and ocean floor beyond national jurisdiction. The first principle declares the area to be the "common heritage" of humanity.

1971: The *International Court of Justice*, in an advisory opinion requested by the Security Council, declares the continued presence of South Africa in Namibia "illegal." The Assembly restores "lawful rights" of the People's Republic of China in the UN. Bahrain becomes independent after the UN helps resolve an Iran-United Kingdom dispute on the status of the territory. Massive UN relief effort aids victims of conflict in East Pakistan (later Bangladesh).

1972: The *UN Environment Conference* meets in Stockholm and adopts a historic declaration on the need for new principles to govern human activities in order to safeguard the natural world. The Assembly sets up the *UN Environment Program* to catalyze action in that regard. The *UN Disaster Relief Organization*, created by the General Assembly to keep tabs on and coordinate international aid in emergencies, becomes operational.

1973: Another war in the Middle East ends with new UN peacekeeping forces in the Sinal and the Golan heights. The Assembly bases the *UN University* in Tokyo to coordinate and marshal efforts by the world's intellectual communities to deal with global problems.

1974: After a breakdown of the world monetary system of fixed currency exchange values, amidst energy and food crises, the Assembly calls for a New International Economic Order as a stable basis for interdependent world economy. World conferences on population and food assess the current situation and underline need for a global change. Inter-communal talks in Cyprus are convoked by the Secretary-General

1975: The *World Conference of the International Women's Year* convenes in Mexico City and adopts the *Declaration on Equality of Women and Their Contribution to Development and Peace*. A Plan of Action for the next ten years provides for world conferences to review progress at the mid-point and end of the *UN Decade for Women*.

1976: To deal with perennial problems of low and erratic prices of raw materials in world trade (on which most developing countries depend), the *UN Conference on Trade and Development* adopts the Integrated Program involving a new fund to finance buffer stocks and a range of individual commodity agreements. A world conference on human habitat plans action.

1977: The Security Council makes the arms embargo against South Africa mandatory. The billion-dollar *International Fund for Agricultural Development*, a new UN specialized agency, begins to finance food production in developing countries.

1978: The General Assembly convenes in special session, for the first time on the topic of disarmament, and succeeds in drawing up a framework for future action and a set of priorities. The Security Council adopts a plan put forward by five Western countries for the independence of Namibia. A UN peacekeeping force is sent to Lebanon.

1979: The General Assembly adopts the *Convention on the Elimination of Discrimination Against Women*, covering political, economic, social, cultural, and civil rights.

1980: As the result of an international campaign coordinated by the *World Health Organization*, smallpox is totally eradicated from the world. The cost of the program to WHO is about what the world spends on arms in three hours.

1981: The General Assembly adopts a *Declaration on Elimination of All Forms of Intolerance and Discrimination Based on Religion or Belief*. The *Conference on New and Renewable Sources of Energy* maps action.

1982: After nine years of complex and painstaking work, the Conference convened by the Assembly adopts what could be the most significant legal instrument of the century, the wide-ranging *Convention on the Law of the Sea*. Secretary-General Perez de Cuellar's first annual report to the Assembly warns of a trend toward world anarchy and urges rededication to Charter principles on the use of the UN as an instrument for peace and rational change. A first *World Conference on Climate* is convened.

1983: The Secretary-General visits southern Africa to consult on how the Security Council plan for independence of Namibia can be implemented. Virtually all outstanding issues are resolved, but South Africa's insistence on the withdrawal of Cuban troops from neighboring Angola before implementation of the plan makes its initiation impossible.

1984: After seven years of work in the *Commission on Human Rights*, the General Assembly adopts the *Convention Against Torture*, hailed as a major step toward creating a more humane world. The Assembly also adopts the Declaration on the critical economic situation and famine in Africa.

1985: The *Office for Emergency Operations*, created by the Secretary-General, spearheads a massive famine relief effort in Africa.

1986: The UN mobilizes a massive international aid program for drought-stricken African countries. In the aftermath of the Chernobyl accident, the *International Atomic Energy Agency* of the UN adopts two international conventions on early notification of atomic accidents and emergency mutual assistance. The Secretary-General of the UN successfully mediates the problem between New Zealand and France about the sinking of a Greenpeace boat.

1987: The *UN Environment Program* obtains international agreement and signature of a world convention on the protection of the ozonosphere. The UN convenes the first world conference on drug abuse and control of illicit traffic of drugs.

1988: The UN helps to bring about the withdrawal of Soviet troops from Afghanistan and to halt the fighting between Iran and Iraq. **UN Peacekeeping Forces** monitor the situation. They are awarded the **Nobel Peace Prize**. The *UN Convention Against Illicit Traffic in Narcotic Drugs* is adopted in December.

1989: The UN establishes a special trust fund to enable even poor nations to bring disputes before the World Court. In January, 149 States unanimously call for the elimination of all chemical weapons. Plans are made for a conference in 1990 to deal with the problems of converting from military to civilian production. Steps are taken by the Secretary-General to ensure that Namibia will finally receive its independence in 1990. The General Assembly declares 1990-2000 the *Decade of International Law*. A second *World Conference on Climate* is convened.

1990: The Security Council, in an unprecedented and unanimous enforcement of the rule of law, imposed an escalating series of economic sanctions against Iraq for its August invasion of Kuwait. The UN, led by its Secretary-General, after years of effort helped to halt the fighting in Nicaragua, to bring independence to Namibia and to move South Africa away from its inhumane support of apartheid. The *World Summit for Children*, organized by the UN, brought over 70 world leaders together in October in an effort to save the lives of millions of children who now perish needlessly each year. The *International Law Commission* and the *UN Legal Committee* resumed consideration of an International Criminal Court to deal with drug trafficking and other international crimes.

1991: The end of the cold war brings about the first destruction of atomic weapons. Several peace negotiations of the UN are crowned with success in Central America and in Africa. The French government suspends nuclear tests.

1992: The UN Security Council meets for the first time ever at the heads of state level. UN peace-keeping forces are used for the first time in an internal conflict (Yugoslavia). Sixteen new member states enter the UN in 1991-92 as a result of the political changes in Eastern Europe.

*   *
*

APPENDIX 2

The UN System

The mere list of the United Nations specialized agencies and world programs, which compose the UN system, illustrates the vastness of today's world cooperation. No other living species has ever so equipped itself with global instruments designed to study, observe, monitor and preserve its habitat. In innumerable organs, meetings and conferences, through thousands of experts and delegates, backed by forty thousand world servants, humankind is today probing its entire biosphere and condition, trying to create peace, to reduce conflicts and tensions, to build bridges and to seek ways for a greater fulfillment of human life to an extent which no philosopher, prophet or social reformer would have ever dreamed possible.

For assistance in visualizing the United Nations System and general information about contacting the UN, the following list has been prepared utilizing various UN directories and *"Essays on Education: A Vision for Educators"*,[38]

The United Nations System:

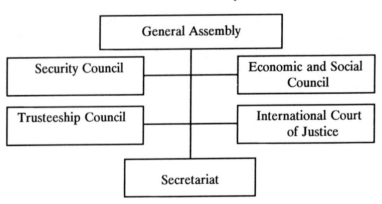

---

[38]   Edited by Joanne Dufour (1992, World Happiness and Cooperation)

Address Information

United Nations Headquarters:
United Nations
New York, NY. 10017   Tel: (212) 963-1234
U.S.A.

United Nations Office at Geneva:
Office des Nations Unies à Geneve
Palais des Nations
CH-1211 Geneva 10   Tel: (41) (22) 734 60 11
Switzerland   FAX: (41) (22) 733 98 79

United Nations Office at Vienna:
Office des Nations Unies à Vienne
Vienna International Centre
P.O. Box 500   Tel: (43) (1) 211.31
A-1400 Vienna, Austria   ("0" for switchboard)

United Nations Office at Nairobi
P.O. Box 30030   Tel: (254) (2) 333930
Nairobi   or 520380
Kenya   FAX: (254) (2) 520724

International Court of Justice
Peace Palace
2517 KJ   The Hague   Tel: (31) (70) 392 44 41
The Netherlands   FAX: (31) (70) 364 99 28

*

Specialized Agencies

International Atomic Energy Agency:
IAEA
P.O. Box 100
Vienna International Centre
A-1400 Vienna,
Austria

Tel: (43) (1) 2360-0
(for switchboard)
FAX: (43) (1) 2345-64

IAEA Liaison Office with the UN
United Nations, DC1-1155
New York, NY, 10017
U.S.A.

Tel: (212) 963-6010
/ 6011
FAX; (212) 751-4117

International Labour Organization
ILO
4, route des Morillons
CH-1211 Geneva 22,
Switzerland

Tel: (41) (22) 799 61 11
FAX: (41) (22) 798 86 85

ILO Liaison Office with the UN
Documents Distribution, ILO Box First Basement
220 East 42nd Street, Suite 3101
New York, NY, 10017-5806
U.S.A.

Tel: (212) 697-0150
/ 0151 / 0153
FAX: (212) 883-0844-85

Food and Agriculture Organization:
FAO
Via delle Terme di Caracalla
00100 Rome,
Italy

Tel: (39) (6) 57971
FAX: (39) (6) 5146.172
5797.3152

FAO Liaison Office with the UN
One United Nations Plaza, Suite DC1-1125
New York, NY. 10017
U.S.A.

Tel: (212) 963-6036
/ 6007
Fax: (212) 888-6188

United Nations, Educational Scientific and Cultural Organization:
UNESCO
7, place de Fontenoy
75700 Paris, France

Tel: (33) (1) 45-68-10-00
FAX: (33) (1) 45-67-16-90

UNESCO - Office for Liaison with the UN
Two United Nations Plaza, Room 900
New York, NY. 10017
U.S.A.

Tel: (212) 963-5984
/ 0185
FAX: (212) 355-5627

World Health Organization:
WHO
20, avenue Appia
1211 Geneva 27,
Switzerland

Tel: (41) (22) 791 21 11

WHO Office at the UN (WHO/UN)
Two United Nations Plaza, DC2- Room 0970
New York, NY. 10017
U.S.A.

Tel: (212) 963-4388
FAX: (212) 223-2920

International Bank for Reconstruction and Development - **IBRD**
(World Bank - also;)

International Finance Corporation; - **IFC**

International Development Association - **IDA**

1818 H Street, N.W.
Washington D.C. 20433
U.S.A.

Tel: (202) 477-1234
FAX: (202) 477-6391

World Bank Office with the United Nations
747 Third Avenue, 26th Floor
New York, NY. 10017
U.S.A.

Tel: (212) 963-6008
FAX: (212) 308 5320

International Monetary Fund:
IMF
700 19th Street, N.W.   Tel: (202) 623-7000
Washington, D.C. 20431   FAX: (202) 623-4661
U.S.A.

International Civil Aviation Organization:
ICAO
1000 Sherbrooke Street West
Montreal, Quebec H3A 2R2   Tel: (514) 285-8219
Canada   FAX: (514) 288-4772

Universal Postal Union:
UPD
Case postale No. 3000
Berne 15,   Tel: (41) (31) 43 22 11
Switzerland   FAX: (41) (31) 43 22 10

International Telecommunication Union:
ITU
Place des Nations
CH-1211 Geneva 20   Tel: (41) (22) 730 51 11
Switzerland   FAX: (41) (22) 733 72 56

World Meteorological Organization:
WMO
41, avenue Giuseppe-Motta
case postale No. 2300
CH-1211 Geneva 2   Tel: (41) (22) 730 81 11
Switzerland   FAX: (41) (22) 734 23 26

International Maritime Organization:
IMO
4 Albert Embankment
London, SE1 7SR   Tel: (44) (71) 735 7611
England   FAX: (44) (71) 587 3210

General Agreement on Tariffs and Trade:
GATT
Centre William Rappard
154, rue de Lausanne
CH-1202 Geneva 21
Switzerland

Tel: (41) (22) 739 51 11
FAX: (41) (22) 731 42 06

World Intellectual Property Organization:
WIPO
34 chemin des Colombettes
1211 Geneva 20,
Switzerland

Tel: (41) (22) 730 91 11
FAX: (41) (22) 733 54 28

WIPO Liaison Office with the UN
Two United Nations Plaza, Room DC2-560
New York, NY. 10017
U.S.A.

Tel: (212) 963-6813
FAX: (212) 963-4801

International Fund for Agricultural Development:
IFAD
Via del Serafico 107
00142 Rome,
Italy

Tel: (39) (6) 54591
FAX: (39) (6) 50434-63

IFAD Liaison Office with the UN
United Nations, Room s-2955 B
New York, NY. 10017
U.S.A.

Tel: (212) 963-4245
FAX: (212) 963-4444

World Tourism Organization:
WTO
Capitán Haya, 42
28020 - Madrid
Spain

Tel: (34) (1) 571 06 28
FAX: (34) (1) 571 37 33

*

Special World Programs

United Nations International Children's Emergency Fund:
UNICEF
Three United Nations Plaza   Tel: (212) 326-7000
New York, NY. 10017   (switchboard)
U.S.A.   FAX: (212) 888-7465

United Nations Conference on Trade and Development:
UNCTAD
Palais des Nations
CH-1211 Geneva 10   Tel: (41) (22) 734 60 11
Switzerland   FAX: (41) (22) 733 65 42

United Nations Development Program:
UNDP
One United Nations Plaza   Tel: (212) 906-5000
New York, NY. 10017   (switchboard)
U.S.A.   FAX: (212) 826-2057

Office of UN Disaster Relief Co-ordinator:
UNDRO
Palais des Nations
CH-1211 Geneva 10   Tel: (41) (22) 734 60 11
Switzerland   FAX: (41) (22) 733 56 23

United Nations Environment Program:
UNEP
P.O. Box 30552
Nairobi   Tel: (254) (2) 333930
Kenya   FAX: (254) (2) 529711

United Nations International Drug Control Programme:
UNDCP
Vienna International Centre
P.O. Box 500
A-1400 Vienna,   Tel: (43) (1) 211 31 0
Austria   FAX: (43) (1) 230 70 02

Office of the United Nations High Commissioner for Refugees:
UNHCR
Centre William Rappard
154 rue de Lausanne
CH-1202 Geneva 21
Switzerland   Tel: (41) (22) 739 81 11

United Nations Industrial Development Organization:
UNIDO
Wagramerstrasse 5   Tel: (43) (1) 211 31 0
1220 Vienna,   (switchboard)
Austria   FAX: (43) (1) 232 15 6

UNIDO Office at New York
One United Nations Plaza, Room DC1-1110 Tel: (212) 963-6890
New York, NY. 10017   / 6882
U.S.A.   FAX: (212) 963-7904

United Nations Institute for Training and Research:
UNITAR
801 United Nations Plaza   Tel: (212) 963-8621
New York, NY. 10017   / 8622
U.S.A.   FAX: (212) 697-8660

United Nations Population Fund:
UNFPA
220 East 42nd Street
New York, NY. 10017-5880   Tel: (212) 297-5000
U.S.A.   FAX: (212) 370-0201

United Nations Relief and Works Agency:
UNRWA
Vienna International Centre
P.O.Box 700
A-1400 Vienna   Tel: (43) (1) 21131
Austria   FAX: (43) (1) 23074-87

United Nations Volunteers:
UNV
Palais des Nations
CH-1211 Geneva 10   Tel: (41) (22) 788 24 55
Switzerland   FAX: (41) (22) 788 25 01

World Food Program:
WFP
Via Cristoforo Colombo, 426   Tel: (39) (6) 57971
00145 Rome   FAX: (39) (6) 57975-652
Italy   / 51335-37

*

United Nations Economic Commissions

Economic Commission for Africa:
ECA
P.O. Box 3001
Addis Ababa
Ethiopia   Tel: (251) (1) 51-72 00

Economic Commission for Europe:
ECE
Palais des Nations
1211 Geneva 10   Tel: (41) (22) 734 60 11
Switzerland   FAX: (41) (22) 734 9825

Economic Commission for Latin America:
ECLAC
Edificio Naciones Unidas
Avenida Dag Hammarskjöld s/n   Tel: (56) (2) 2085051
Vitacura   (to 2085061)
Casilla 179-D   FAX: (56) (2) 2080252
Santiago, Chile   (56) (2) 2081946

Economic and Social Commission for Asia and the Pacific:
ESCAP
United Nations Building
Rajdamnern Avenue   Tel: (66) (2) 2829161-200
Bangkok 10200   (66) (2) 2829381-389
Thailand   FAX: (66) (2) 2829602

Economic and Social Commission for Western Asia:
ESCWA - (Temporary Headquarters)
28 Abdul Hamid Sharaf Street   Tel: (962) (6) 694351
Shmeisani   (8 lines)
(Mailing address)   FAX: (962) (6) 694980
P.O. Box 927115   /694981
Amman, Jordan   /694982

*

Universities and Educational Institutions

United Nations University:
UNU
Toho Seimei Building
15-1 Shibuya 2-chome
Shibuya-ku
Tokyo 150   Tel: (81) (3) 3499 2811
Japan   FAX: (81) (3) 3499 2828

United Nations University: (cont.)
UNU - North America
United Nations
Room DC2-1462   Tel: (212) 963-6387
New York, NY. 10017   FAX: (212) 371-9454

UNU - Europe
c/o **UNESCO** Rooms 7B 111-113
1, Rue Miollis   Tel: (33) (1) 45 68 30 07
75732 Paris Cedex 15   (ext.10)
France   FAX: (33) (1) 40 65 91 86

International Centre for Theoretical Physics:
c/o **IAEA** or
P.O. Box 586
Stada Costiera 11, Miramare, Trieste   Tel: (39) (40) 22 40 1
Italy   FAX: (39) (40) 22 41 63

International Maritime University:
Malmö, Sweden
c/o **IMO**
4 Albert Embankment
London, SE1 7SR   Tel: (44) (71) 735 7611
England   FAX: (44) (71) 587 3210

International Research and Training
Institute for the Advancement of Women:
INSTRAW
Calle César Nicolás Penson 102-A
P.O. Box 21747
Santo Domingo   Tel: (500) (809) 685-2111/7
Dominican Republic   FAX: (500) (809) 685-2117

INSTRAW - New York Liaison Office
c/o United Nations
Room S-3094   Tel: (212) 963-5684
New York, NY. 10017   FAX: (212) 963-2978

University for Peace
UNIPAZ
P.O. Box 138
Ciudad Colón   Tel: (506) 49 10 72
Costa Rica   FAX: (506) 49 19 29

*

Radio for Peace International, the international short-wave broadcasting station operates from the campus of the University for Peace. Programing includes a large variety of subjects relating to peace, including programs from the United Nations and UNESCO radio services. The short-wave frequencies used by Radio for Peace International are 21.565 - 13.360 and 7.375 MHz. For more information write to:

Radio for Peace International

P.O. Box 88
Santa Ana   Tel: (506) 49 18 21
Costa Rica   FAX: (506) 49 19 29

and/or

P.O. Box 10869-B
Eugene, OR. 97440   Tel: (503) 741-1794
U.S.A.   FAX: (503) 741-1279

*

The United Nations, its Specialized Agencies and World Programs all have information departments or offices at the addresses above. The United Nations also has information centers in most capitals of the world. Consult your local telephone directory or write to the:

UN Information Centers Division
Department of Public Information
Room S-1060 A
United Nations
New York, NY. 10017   Tel: (212) 963-0798

Many Non-Government Organizations (**NGO**) accredited with the United Nations provide information on their activities of special interest in conjunction with the UN System. For information in your particular field of interest, write to the:

NGO and Institutional Relations Section
Department of Public Information
Room S-1037 D
United Nations
New York, NY. 10017   Tel: (212) 963-6842

In most countries and larger cities there are branches of the United Nations Associations (**UNA**). Local chapters are able to provide information about the United Nations' System. Anyone may join the UNA and new members are always welcome. For information about the UNA or the location of regional branches write to the:

World Federation of United Nations Associations:
WFUNA
Palais des Nations
CH-1211 Geneva 10
Switzerland

   - or -

WFUNA Liaison Office
United Nations
Room DC1-1177
New York, NY. 10017   Tel: (212) 963-5610

For information regarding existing United Nations Associations in the United States, about creating a new branch or information about model UN programs for schools and universities write to:

The United Nations Association of the United States
485 Fifth Avenue
New York, Ny. 10017   Tel: (212) 697-3232

* *
*

APPENDIX 3

United Nations World Conferences
and Special Observances

I reproduce here, a list of world conferences and special observances decided so far by the United Nations and its agencies. They are the best and most direct way for the citizens of this planet to take part and enhance the global consciousness of the human family, so urgently needed at this juncture of evolution. I wish that these days be mentioned on calendars, that school children would join in activities on such days and that the issues of these days be discussed in the family, in professions, in business, in communities, and in national governments.

I have suggested many ideas in my various books on what people can do for peace and a better world. Global conferences and observances are the simplest, most direct way for people to participate in the building of a better world. These observed days provide a good selection of subjects to choose from according to sex, age, inclinations and professional activities. I beg therefore every reader to select at least one of these celebrations and to make it his or her duty to do something special on that day. Here is the list.[39]

International Conferences

1992	United Nations Conference on the Environment and Development
1993	World Conference on Human Rights
1994	International Conference on Population and Development
1995	Fourth World Conference on women Fiftieth Anniversary of the United Nations

*

---

[39]   See chapter 10, Global Celebrations, pages 93 - 103, in my book entitled, *"The Birth of a Global Civilization"*, (1991, World Happiness and Cooperation)

International Decades

1983 - 1992	United Nations Decade of Disabled Persons
1983 - 1992	Second Decade to Combat Racism and Racial Discrimination
1985 - 1994	Transport and Communications Decade for Asia and the Pacific
1988 - 1997	World Decade for Cultural Development
1990's	International Decade for Natural Disaster Reduction Third Disarmament Decade
1990 - 2000	International Decade for the Eradication of Colonialism Second Transport and Communications Decade in Africa Fourth United Nations Development Decade Decade of International Law

*

International Years

1992	International Year of Space
1993	International Year of the World's Indigenous People
1994	International Year of the Family

*

International Days and Weeks

8 March	International Women's Day
21 March	International Day for the Elimination of Racial Discrimination
23 March	World Meteorological Day
7 April	World Health Day
17 May	World Telecommunication Day
Beginning 25 May	Week of Solidarity with the Peoples Struggling against Racism and Racial Discrimination
31 May	World No-Tobacco Day
4 June	International Day of Innocent Children Victims of Aggression
5 June	World Environment Day
16 June	International Day of Solidarity with the Struggling People of South Africa
26 June	International Day against Drug Abuse and Illicit Trafficking
11 July	World Population Day
9 August	International Day of Solidarity with the Struggle of Women in South Africa and Namibia
8 September	International Literacy Day

3rd Tuesday of September	International Day of Peace (Opening of the UN General Assembly)
During the last week of September	World Maritime Day
1 October	International Day for the Elderly
1st Monday of October	Universal Children's Day and World Habitat Day
9 October	World Post Day
2nd Wednesday of October	International Day for Natural Disaster Reduction
11 October	Day of Solidarity with South African Political Prisoners
16 October	World Food Day
24 October	United Nations' Day and World Development Information Day
24-30 October	Disarmament Week
Week of 11 November	International Week of Science and Peace
20 November	Africa Industrialization Day
29 November	International Day of Solidarity with the Palestinian People
1 December	World AIDS Day
5 December	International Volunteer Day for Economic and Social Development
10 December	Human Rights Day

*

Join in these global celebrations and programs[40] by creating your own special activities.   For information contact the:

Public Inquiries Unit
United Nations
Room GA-57
New York, NY   10017   Telephone (212) 963-4475

One of the best ways to recognize global celebrations and programs as well as to promote the United Nations is to display the UN flag. Whether it be at home, in school or work, or simply in the course of your daily activies the UN flag is an attracive reminder of our global heritage.   UN flags may be obtained from the following sources:

Individual UN flag stickers;
Hammond Publishing Co.,Inc.
G-7166 Saginaw St.
P.O. Box 279   Tel: (313) 686-8881
Mt. Morris, MI. 48458   FAX: (313) 686-0561
U.S.A.

Desk and full size flags;
United Nations Gift Shop   United Nations Gift Shop
Rm. GA 32-A   Palais des Nations
United Nations, NY. 10017   CH-1211 Geneva 10
U.S.A.   Switzerland

World Happiness and Cooperation
P.O. Box 1153
Anacortes, WA. 98221
U.S.A.
                          *   *
                              *

---

[40]   From "*Basic Facts About the United Nations*", Sales Publication E.90. 1.2, obtainable from the United Nations Bookshop, Room GA-32-B, United Nations, New York, NY. 100017 (212) 963-7680

WORKS BY ROBERT MULLER

English

A Planet of Hope   (World Happiness and Cooperation, U.S.)

Decide To   (World Happiness and Cooperation, U.S.)

Dialogues of Hope   (World Happiness and Cooperation, U.S.)

Essays on Education, A Vision for Educators, edited by Joanne Dufour
   (World Happiness and Cooperation, U.S.)

First Lady of the World   (World Happiness and Cooperation, U.S.)

Most of All, They Taught Me Happiness   (Doubleday and World
   Happiness and Cooperation, U.S.)

My Testament to the UN (World Happiness and Cooperation, U.S.)

New Genesis, Shaping a Global Spriituality   (World Happiness and
   Cooperation, U.S.)

*Planetary Conciousness in the Thought of Teilhard de Chardin and
Robert Muller, with a proposal for a Bimillenium celebration of life*
   by Margaret McGurn,   (World Happiness and Cooperation, U.S.)

What War Taught Me About Peace, with a Peace Plan 2010
   (Doubleday, U.S.)

World Joke Book, Vol. 1 (World Happiness and Cooperation, U.S.)

The World Core Curriculum in the Robert Muller School   (Robert
   Muller School, Arlington, Texas, U.S.)

WORKS BY ROBERT MULLER

German

Ich Lernte zu Leben (translation of *Most of All They* ...)
(Dianus-Trikont, Munich, Germany)

Die Neuerschaffung der Welt (translation of *New Genesis* ...)
(Goldman Verlag, Munich, Germany)

Planet der Hoffnung (German edition of *Planet of Hope*)
(Goldman Verlag, Munich, Germany)

French

Sima mon Amour - an international novel in French, Erckman -
Chartrian literary prize, 1983, (Éditions Pierron,
Sarreguemines, France)

Au Bonheur, à l'Amour, à la Paix (translation of *New Genesis* ...)
(Éditions Pierron, Sarreguemines, France)

Spanish

Hacia el Planeta de Dios, diálogos con Robert Muller, by Hilda
Berger, (Lima, Peru)

Portuguese

Decida - Se (translation of *Decide To*)
(Editora Aquariana Ltda, São Paulo, Brasil)

Polish

New Genesis ... Polish translation Instytut Wysawniczy
(Warsaw, Poland)

Japanese

New Genesis ..., Japanese edition, University of the Sacred Heart
(Catholic Press Center, Tokyo, Japan)

* *

*